ON THE FRONT LINES

The Lay Person in the Church After Vatican II

Jordan Aumann, O.P.

Wipf and Stock Publishers
150 West Broadway • Eugene OR 97401
2000

On the Front Lines

By Aumann, Jordan
Copyright©1990 by Aumann, Jordan

Reprinted by *Wipf and Stock Publishers*
150 West Broadway • Eugene OR 97401

Previously published by Alba House, 1990.

Nihil Obstat:
Reverend George J. Dyer, S.T.D.
Censor Deputatus

Imprimi Potest:
Reverend Dennis R. Zusy, O.P.
Vicar Provincial

Imprimatur:
Reverend James P. Roache
Vicar General
Archdiocese of Chicago
August 27, 1989

The Nihil Obstat and Imprimatur are
official declarations that a book or pamphlet is free
of doctrinal or moral error. No implication is contained therein
that those who have granted the Nihil Obstat and
Imprimatur agree with the contents,
opinions, or statements expressed.

''The faithful, more precisely the lay faithful, find themselves *on the front lines* of the Church's life; for them the Church is the animating principle for human society. Therefore, they in particular ought to have an ever clearer consciousness not only of belonging to the Church, but of being the Church; that is to say, the community of the faithful on earth under the leadership of the Pope, the head of all, and of the bishops in communion with him. These are the Church.''
(Pope Pius XII, February 20, 1946)

CONTENTS

PREFACE

This book is written for you, the laity, because you are the Church.
Indeed, everything in the Church — the preaching of the Gospel,
the administration of the sacraments, the liturgical assembly, the
service of the clergy — it is all for you. For too long you have been
the passive, silent majority in the Church, and even now we are
witnessing a reluctance of many Christians to engage in full, active
membership in the Church. Of course, we must also recognize the
fact that sometimes the laity have been pushed aside by the clergy
who more and more in recent years have taken over the realm of
politics and social questions.

In the past two decades, however, the laity have been called
upon to take their rightful place in the Church and in the world. The
Second Vatican Council issued a special document addressed to the
laity and twenty years later the 1987 Synod on the Laity studied in
depth the vocation and mission of the lay person in the Church.
Most recently Pope John Paul II issued his exhortation to the laity
(December 30, 1988), based on the findings and recommendations
of the 1987 Synod.

In the intervening years since the close of the Second Vatican
Council there has been an increasing tension and division in the
Church, due to the inability or unwillingness of some Catholics to
make the adjustments and adaptations suggested by Vatican
Council II and, on the other hand, the tendency of others to go far
beyond what the Council had envisaged. By this time we have in
the Church a rather well-defined dualism as regards the nature of

the Church and the various ecclesiastical ministries. We have, on the one hand, what we could call the traditional concept of the Church as a visible society with an authoritative head to whom all the members owe obedience; it is an institutional, hierarchical concept of the Church. On the other hand, there are those who see the Church as a community of believers who enjoy certain God-given rights and for whom the conscience of the individual rather than obedience to authority is the ultimate determinant.

In his Apostolic Exhortation, addressed to the laity, Pope John Paul II made "a strong appeal to one and all, pastors and faithful, never to become tired of maintaining . . . an ecclesial consciousness, which is ever mindful of what it means to be members of the Church of Jesus Christ, participants in her mystery of communion and in her dynamism in mission and the aposto-late. . . . A real sense of Church communion, the gift of the Spirit that urges our free and generous response, will bring forth as its precious fruit in the 'one and catholic' Church the continuing value of the rich variety of vocations and conditions of life, charisms, ministries, works and responsibilities, as well as a more demon-strable and decisive collaboration of groups, associations and movements of the lay faithful in keeping with the accomplishment of the commonly shared salvific mission of the Church herself. This communion is already in itself the first great sign in the world of the presence of Christ, the Savior. At the same time, it promotes and stimulates the proper apostolic and missionary action of the Church. . . . A great venture, both challenging and wonderful, is entrusted to the Church — that of a re-evangelization, which is so much needed by the present world. The lay faithful ought to regard themselves as an active and responsible part of this venture, called as they are to proclaim and to live the gospel in service to the person and to society while respecting the totality of the values and needs of both."

In our discussion of the role of the laity in the Church and in the world we shall follow closely the teachings of the Second

Vatican Council, the legislation of the revised *Code of Canon Law*, and the various documents that have been promulgated concerning lay participation in the life and mission of the Church. For that reason the text is heavily laden with quotations, and deliberately so, because we are presuming that the majority of the laity do not have ready access to those important sources. At the same time we shall take into account the various questions that are still under study by commissions that have been established for that purpose. Consequently, the last word has not yet been spoken or written concerning the role of the laity, but we already have ample material that should challenge the lay Christians to give witness to the Gospel in their personal lives and to Christianize their domestic and social milieu.

Jordan Aumann, O.P.

ACKNOWLEDGMENTS

We wish to acknowledge the following sources for quotations that appear throughout this work:

Vatican Council II: The Conciliar and Post Conciliar Documents, edited by Austin Flannery, O.P., Liturgical Press, Collegeville, Minnesota, 1975. *Vatican Council II: More Post Conciliar Documents*, edited by Austin Flannery, O.P., Dominican Publications, Dublin, 1982.

The Code of Canon Law, published by Collins Liturgical Publications, London, 1983.

Apostolic Exhortation, "Christifideles Laici," Vatican Polyglot Press, Vatican City, 1988.

ABBREVIATIONS

AA - *Apostolicam Actuositatem*: Decree on the Apostolate of Lay People, 1965.

AAS - *Acta Apostolicae Sedis*: Official Publication of Vatican Documents.

AG - *Ad Gentes Divinitus*: Decree on the Church's Missionary Activity, 1965.

CD - *Christus Dominus*: Decree on the Pastoral Office of Bishops in the Church, 1965.

CL - *Christifideles Laici*: Apostolic Exhortation on the Vocation and the Mission of the Laity in the Church and in the World, 1988.

CT - *Catechesi Tradendae*: Catechesis in Our Time, 1979.

CU - *Convenientes ex Universo*: Justice in the World, 1971.

FC - *Familiaris Consortio*: The Christian Family in the Modern World, 1981.

GE - *Gravissimum Educationis*: Declaration on Christian Education, 1965.

GS - *Gaudium et Spes*: Pastoral Constitution on the Church in the Modern World, 1965.

IO - *Inter Oecumenici*: Instruction on the Liturgy, 1964.

LG - *Lumen Gentium*: Dogmatic Constitution on the Church, 1964.

MC - *Mystici Corporis*: Encyclical Letter on the Church, 1943.

MQ - *Ministeria Quaedam*: Apostolic Letter on First Tonsure, Minor Orders and the Subdiaconate, 1972.

NA - *Nostra Aetate*: Declaration on the Church's Relations with non-Christian Religions, 1965.

SC - *Sacrosanctum Concilium*: Constitution on the Sacred Liturgy, 1963.

UR - *Unitatis Redintegratio*: Decree on Ecumenism, 1964.

USCC - *United States Catholic Conference*, Washington, D.C.

ON THE
FRONT LINES

CHAPTER 1

THE NATURE AND MISSION OF THE CHURCH

If we mention the government of the United States to the average citizen, he or she will most likely think immediately of Washington, D.C., or the President, the Congress and the Supreme Court. Similarly, if we say "the Catholic Church," many persons will automatically think of the Vatican in Rome, the Pope or perhaps their local bishop. In both cases, however, the identification will be inaccurate.

We do sometimes think in those categories, and rightly so, as when we discuss the government's foreign policy, the laws passed by Congress, or the services provided by the government. The same thing holds true of the concept of the Catholic Church when we ask what the Church teaches or when we refer to the canon law of the Church, the documents of the Second Vatican Council or an encyclical issued by the Holy Father. The executive, legislative and judicial branches of the government and of the Church rightly enjoy a certain priority in leadership and service.

But a government without citizens and a Church without membership would be like a head without a body. Consequently, as a democracy, the United States of America is governed ultimately by its citizens, who legislate through their elected delegates in Congress. The Constitution of the United States makes this very clear when it begins with the words: "We, the people." The Catholic Church, on the other hand, is not a democracy in the strict sense of the word; nevertheless, those who hold authority in the Church are under serious obligation to serve its members and to promote the common good of the Church. Christ himself commanded this when, after washing the feet of the apostles at the Last Supper, he said: "But if I washed your feet — I who am Teacher and Lord — then you must wash each other's feet. What I just did was to give you an example: as I have done, so you must do" (Jn 13:14-15).

The hierarchy alone — Pope and bishops — are not the Church, though they have an authoritative position in the Church. For a complete and accurate concept of the Church we must include all of its members, from the Pope down to the most recently baptized infant. But the Church is a very complex reality, indeed it is a mystery, and therefore it is very difficult to describe its nature and reality in a definition. So we use images or symbols, as are found in the Bible, for example: the kingdom of God, the sheepfold, the tree that grows from a small seed, the vine and the branches, discipleship. The value of such images is that we do get at least a partial comprehension of what the Church is, although they may not all be meaningful to people of every nation and culture. Theologians also have attempted to discover the word or image that would best portray the reality of the Church and they have offered us such terms as institution, sacrament, community, pilgrim people, household of the Lord, assembly, or fellowship with God and with one another in Christ. Some of the foregoing terms are powerful and inspiring but not all of them are clear and exact enough to be appreciated by all Christians; some of them, in fact, may be unacceptable to contemporary Catholics or may lead to misunderstanding.

Fortunately for us, the Second Vatican Council treated at length of the Church in its basic document, the *Dogmatic Constitution on the Church*. At the very outset the Fathers of the Council spoke of the "mystery of the Church" and then used a variety of symbols to portray it. Thus, the Church is a sacrament, "a sign and instrument of communion with God and of unity among all people"; it is the kingdom of Christ; a people brought into unity from the unity of the Father, the Son and the Holy Spirit; the Church is our mother; the Church is the body of Christ. The document likewise contains a listing of the descriptions of the Church as given in the Bible. But the two expressions or images of the Church that are especially relevant to our times and, indeed, best suited for a balanced understanding of the nature and mission of the Church are "People of God" and "Mystical Body of Christ."

THE PEOPLE OF GOD

The expression "People of God" is an ancient one. It is found in the Old Testament, and there it means the Jews, the chosen people of God, as distinct from the Gentiles. It is an all-inclusive term that applies to each and every Jew, whether priest or Levite or one of the ordinary people. It is also a term that designates the common bond that linked all the Jews together as a community or race; they are God's chosen people. Thus, we read in the Book of Deuteronomy (it is Moses who speaks):

> Today you are making this agreement with the Lord: he is to be your God and you are to walk in his ways and observe his statutes, commandments and decrees, and to hearken to his voice. And today the Lord is making this agreement with you: you are to be a people peculiarly his own, as he promised you; and provided you keep all his commandments, he will then raise you high in praise and renown and glory above all other nations he has made, and you will be a people sacred to the Lord, your God, as he promised. (Dt 26:17-19)

When we turn to the New Testament we again find the word "people," but this time it applies to the followers of Christ. They are described by St. Peter as "a chosen race, a royal priesthood, a holy nation, a people he claims for his own to proclaim the glorious works of the one who called you from darkness into his marvelous light" (1 P 2:9). Not only are the disciples of Christ a people or a nation set apart from all others; they are also given a mission: to proclaim the glorious works of Christ. The Christians, therefore, cannot, like the Jews, cultivate a separatist mentality because of their status as the chosen people, although in the early days of the Church they did have to withdraw from certain areas of persecution.

In the year 95 or 96, St. Clement of Rome wrote to the Christians of Corinth and referred to them as the "People of God." It had the same meaning as it did for the Jews, namely, that all Christians without exception and from whatever class or condition are God's people. The term used to express this concept was the Greek word "*laos*," which means "people"; but we should note that St. Clement also distinguished between those in holy orders, who have their own special ministries and duties, and the laity, who are to follow the rules laid down for them. By the third century ecclesiastical writers such as St. Cyprian, Tertullian and Origen were using the same word to designate those members of the Church who were not in holy orders. From that time on, the word "lay" or "laity" (*laos*) was no longer applied to all the People of God indiscriminately but only to those Christians who were not members of the clergy.

This restricted use of the word "laity" as applying only to those who are simply baptized Christians but are not in holy orders is a return to the correct etymology of the word "*laos*." In Greek usage before the time of Christ, the word meant all those free citizens who were not engaged in government. Similarly, the Christian laity are all those who are not members of the clergy. But there is something more here than the distinction between two classes of Christians in the Church. The very word "clergy" or "cleric" also comes from the Greek: *"kleros,"* which means one's portion or lot. Thus, we read in Psalm XV: "The Lord is my portion." And that verse describes the Christian who is in holy orders. As a cleric he is totally dedicated to the things of God, while the laity is their secularity.

There are those who have argued that since there was no distinction of classes of Christians in the early Church, but all were equally the People of God, there is no justification for a hierarchy or for dividing the members of the Church into clergy and laity. For them, the Church of Christ should be a Church without class or rank or distinction. Such an opinion is completely without basis. We have already seen that even the etymology of the word *"laos"* is based on the distinction of classes in the democratic Greek society. Moreover, Christ himself called certain disciples to follow him and gave them distinctive ministries and functions, beginning with Peter as the head of the initial hierarchy. Later, St. Paul was equally insistent on the division of charisms, ministries and offices in the Church.

If, then, the term *"laos"* or *"laikos"* was eventually restricted to the simply baptized Christians as distinct from those in holy orders, what terms were used to designate the members of the Church as the People of God? When all Christians were referred to indiscriminately as members of the Church of Christ the following expressions could be used: "brethren," " disciples," "Christ's faithful," or simply "Christians." As we shall see, the revised *Code of Canon Law* chose the expression "Christ's faithful," or "faithful of Christ," as the preferred word to include all the members of the Church. There is a discrepancy here, because the documents of the Second Vatican Council frequently use the term "the faithful" to refer exclusively to the laity, and when treating of all the members of the Church without distinction, as in the second chapter of *Lumen Gentium*, the phrase used is "the People of

God.'' The two expressions are interchangeable, but nevertheless there is a slight difference of meaning between ''People of God'' and ''the faithful of Christ.'' It would perhaps be similar to the difference between the phrases ''the American people'' and ''the citizens of the United States.''

One may ask at this point what is the value of discussing the etymology of words and their change in meaning through the centuries. First of all, if the word ''*laos*'' was originally used to mean the People of God, then the use of this phrase to designate all baptized Christians without exception is not an innovation introduced by the Second Vatican Council but the restoration of a traditional formula that had been neglected or even forgotten. Secondly, since language does evolve and change, the word ''laity'' will not necessarily have the same meaning that it did when first used. We have seen that even in the first century, with St. Clement, this word designated those Christians who were simply baptized but were not in holy orders. Consequently, one cannot use the original meaning of ''*laos*'' to prove that the Church at its beginning was a charismatic, totally democratic community without a hierarchy.

The revival of the description of the Church as the People of God has laid the foundation for the renewal and development of the theology of the Church. If we look back at the ecclesiology promulgated by the Council of Trent (1545-1563), we shall find that it was based on the concept of the Church as a perfect but unequal society. The emphasis was placed on the distinction between the hierarchy and the faithful, ecclesiastical authority and obedience, infallibility in teaching and in believing. As a result, the institutional, hierarchical aspect of the Church received all the attention, and the ordinary faithful were left in the shadows. With all this concentration on ecclesiastical authority and the hierarchy, it was inevitable that the Church would be seen as the domain of the clergy. Of course, there were various factors that led to the so-called ''clericalization'' of the Church, and not least among them was the need to defend the traditional sacramental theology of the Church against the Protestant Reformers. Thus, according to some historians, Martin Luther introduced "congregationalism," that is, control of the churches and pastors by the laity, so that by the time of Calvin and Zwingli the ministry of pastors was for all practical purposes restricted to preaching. We can safely say, however, that no orthodox theologian would ever define the Church exclusively as the hierarchy, but in some of their writings, as in the language of ordinary Christians, it is the hierarchy that comes to mind when one speaks of the Church. Nevertheless, it should be noted that the *Catechism of the Council of Trent* explicitly states that the word "Church" must never be understood as applying only to the hierarchy.

Coming down to the year 1917 and the *Code of Canon Law* promulgated in that same year, we find that the tone is still very clerical. One gets the impression that everything in the Church is concentrated in the hierarchy and that there is an excessive concern with power and authority. The laity are seldom mentioned and, when they are, the inference is that they are purely passive members of the Church who receive whatever they receive, only through the hierarchy. Their active participation in the community of the faithful and in the mission of the Church is for all practical purposes totally ignored.

This mentality prevailed in the Church for the 400 years prior to the Second Vatican Council. But in all fairness, we should acknowledge that what we see as an unwarranted emphasis on the role and authority of the hierarchy in the Church was in some measure a backlash against the excesses committed by the laity in the name of democracy and the unlawful interference of secular rulers in Church affairs. We are referring to the troubles of the Church from the twelfth century until the Protestant Reformation. Pope Boniface VIII (1294-1303) had to issue a strongly worded document in order to defend the rights of the hierarchy and the authority of the Church. The following excerpt is an example of the tone of that document.

> Antiquity has often taught what the experience of the present
> time manifestly demonstrates: that the laity are often enemies of
> the clergy, because, not content with their own limits, they seek
> to obtain that which is forbidden, rejecting that which should
> restrain them in order to obtain that which is not permitted, and
> not judiciously considering that they are forbidden all power
> over clerics or ecclesiastical goods or persons. They rather
> impose heavy burdens on prelates of the Church, on churches
> and ecclesiastical personages, both regulars and seculars.
> (*Clericis laicos*, 1266)

Closer to our own times, Pope Gregory XVI (1831-1846) stated: "No one can deny that the Church is an unequal society in which God has destined some to command and others to obey." Pope Leo XIII (1878-1903) likewise insisted emphatically on the two distinct classes in the Church: pastors and their flocks, the leaders and the people. "The role of the first order," he said, "is to teach, to govern and to lead men in life; to impose rules. The duty of the other is to submit itself to the first, to obey it, to carry out its orders and to honor it." And yet it was this same Pope who said that "when circumstances make it necessary, it is not prelates alone who have to watch over the integrity of the faith; as St. Thomas says, 'Everyone is bound to show forth his faith publicly, whether for the instruction and encouragement of other faithful or to repel the onslaughts of adversaries.' "

Meanwhile Cardinal Newman (1801-1890) made a strong plea for the education of the Catholic laity and even wrote an essay in which he urged that the laity be consulted in matters of doctrine (1859). Due to the climate in Rome at the time the essay was not only ill received but Newman himself was placed under a cloud of suspicion as to his orthodoxy. Monsignor Talbot, who had great influence in Rome, wrote to Cardinal Manning: "If a check is not placed on the laity of England, they will be rulers of the Catholic Church in England instead of the Holy See and the episcopate. . . .

What is the province of the laity? To hunt, to shoot, to entertain. These matters they understand; but to meddle with ecclesiastical matters they have no right at all, and this affair of Newman is a matter purely ecclesiastical. . . . Dr. Newman is the most dangerous man in England, and you will see that he will make use of the laity against Your Grace.''

Fortunately, Cardinal Newman has been amply vindicated by the subsequent teaching on the role of the laity as promulgated by Pope Pius X (1903-1914), Pope Pius XI (1922-1939) and Pope Pius XII (1939-1959). These three Popes were the outstanding promoters of Catholic Action, together with St. Vincent Pallotti (1795-1850), the founder of the Society for Catholic Action, and Monsignor Josemaría Escrivá, the founder of Opus Dei.

We have given this brief historical survey in order to show that there has been a gradual promotion of the laity to a more active participation in the Church in the last two centuries. But with the promulgation of the documents of the Second Vatican Council under Pope Paul VI and the post-Conciliar documents promulgated by Pope John Paul II, and thanks in large measure to the preliminary work of theologians such as Yves Congar, O.P., Raymond Spiazzi, O.P., and Jerome Hamer, O.P., there can no longer be any doubt whatsoever concerning the rights and duties of the laity as members of the People of God. At long last the Church authorities were listening to the voices of theologians like the founder of Opus Dei who, as early as 1932, had made the following statement quoted in the book *Conversations with Monsignor Josemaría Escrivá* (p. 32):

> The prejudice that ordinary members of the faithful must limit themselves to helping the clergy in ecclesiastical apostolates has to be rejected. There is no reason why the secular apostolate should always be a mere participation in the apostolate of the hierarchy. Secular people too have to have a duty to do apostolate; not because they receive a canonical mission, but because

they are part of the Church. Their mission . . . is fulfilled in their profession, their job, their family, and among their colleagues and friends.

[The author of the book then comments as follows:]

Today, after the solemn teachings of Vatican II, it is unlikely that anyone in the Church would question the orthodoxy of this teaching. But how many people have really abandoned the narrow concept of the apostolate of the laity as a pastoral work organized from the top down? How many people have got beyond the previous monolithic concept of the lay apostolate, and understand that it can and indeed should exist without the necessity of rigid centralized structures, canonical missions and hierarchical mandates? How many people who consider the laity as ''the long arm of the Church,'' do not at the same time confuse in their minds the concept of Church — the People of God — with the more limited concept of hierarchy? How many laymen understand that unless they act in tactful communion with the hierarchy, they have no right to claim their legitimate sphere of apostolic autonomy? (*Conversations with Msgr. Josemaría Escrivá*, Dublin, 1968)

Coming now to the Second Vatican Council (1962-1965) and its *Dogmatic Constitution on the Church*, the first thing we note is that there is an entirely new approach to ecclesiology. The Church is presented at the very outset as a mystery, not in the commonly accepted meaning of that word, but as St. Paul used it. Hence, to speak of the mystery of the Church or the Church as a mystery refers to the divine plan of salvation as contained in God's revelation. The Church, instituted by Christ and acting only and always through the merits and the authority of Christ, is the sacrament or instrument through which its members are brought into communion with the Trinity and with each other. Thus, in his Apostolic Exhortation on the vocation and mission of the lay faithful (1988),

Pope John Paul says of the Church: ''She is *mystery* because the very life and love of the Father, Son and Holy Spirit are the gift gratuitously offered to all those who are born of water and the Holy Spirit (cf. Jn 3:5), and called to relive the very *communion* of God and to manifest it and communicate it in history (mission)'' (CL 8). Therefore, in opening the document with the concept of the Church as ''mystery,'' the Council stressed the fact that the origin of the Church is divine, as are the mission and goal of the Church. And although the Church is also a visible, structured society and is therefore institutional, hierarchical and made up of human members, the reality of the Church lies beyond the purely human level. The Church is therefore rightly called a sacrament, because it is a visible sign instituted by Christ to give to its members the divine life of grace and thereby to bring them into communion with the Trinity.

Because of this conjunction of the visible and the invisible, of the human and the divine in the Church, any members of the Church who would withdraw completely from the temporal realities of this world or from love and concern for their neighbors would be unfaithful to their Christian vocation. Conversely, those who would become so involved in the temporal realities of the world as to be concerned only with the socio-economic problems of society, without any explicit relation to Christ, could hardly call themselves authentic Christians. Man does not live by bread alone.

In addition to being described as a mystery and a sacrament, the Church is also called the People of God, and this expression is the one that occurs most frequently in the documents of the Second Vatican Council. We have already seen that it is not an original expression, but one that goes back to the early Church. And when we speak of the Church as the People of God, we are once again touching on the divine and spiritual aspect of the Church as mystery. The People of God are a people chosen by God through Jesus Christ and, though they are in the world, they are called out of the purely temporal order to become the holy People of God. They thus form a community of the faithful in Christ, a community that should first be seen in its totality and universality before one speaks of the various classes of members or the diversity of ministries and offices in the Church. This total or "catholic" view of the Church of Christ is the background against which one can then discuss the community of all the local churches throughout the world under the leadership and care of the Holy Father, the mutual relationship between the hierarchy and the laity, and the interaction of individual Christians among themselves within their particular vocation or condition of life. But if we fix our gaze exclusively on only one element in the Church — the hierarchy or the laity — we won't be able "to see the forest for the trees."

With good reason, therefore, the Second Vatican Council repeatedly referred to the Church as the People of God, a concept that underlines the fact that all the members of the Church have a common legal status and they all share in the one and the same baptism, the same faith, the same grace and the same vocation. Consequently, all the members of the People of God, from the Pope down to the most recently baptized infant, must profess the same creed, make use of the sacraments instituted by Christ, live a life of Christian witness, and take an active part in the mission of the Church according to their state of life. In this respect we are all one in Christ. And it is also because of their common incorporation into Christ through baptism that all Christians, regardless of their state in life, are called to the perfection of charity. The People of God should be a holy people because they are God's people.

If one were to ask now what is the precise basis for the equality of all the members of the People of God, the answer would be that it is rooted in the one thing that all Christians have in common: their incorporation into Christ through baptism of water and the Holy Spirit. For that reason, St. Paul could say: "Each one of you is a son of God because of your faith in Christ Jesus. All of you who have been baptized into Christ have clothed yourselves with him. There does not exist among you Jew or Greek, slave or freeman, male or female. All are one in Christ Jesus" (Gal 3:26-29). If, therefore, there are any distinctions among the members of the People of God, they will have to come from some other source, from something that has been added to their baptismal commitment.

As a consequence of the basic equality of all baptized Christians the aspect of "*communio*" or "*koinonia*" follows logically. But we should be careful not to confuse that "*communio*" with the sociological concept of community, meaning a group of like-minded persons seeking the same goal or simply a society. The Church, of course, is a visible society, but when we speak of the Church as the People of God we should be thinking rather of the Church as communion.

What does it mean to say that the Church is communion? If we look at a dictionary we shall find that communion is defined as "a possessing or sharing in common; a participation." And this meaning also applies to a religious fellowship. We may say, therefore, that there must first be communion before there can be community. This is evident from the account of the early Church as given in the Acts of the Apostles. Sharing as they did in one and the same faith and baptism, "the community of believers were of one heart and one mind" (Acts 4:32). Being like-minded persons in a faith community, the early Christians gave expression to their fellowship or communion by faithful adherence to the teaching of the apostles, frequent celebration of the Eucharist, daily prayer in common and the practice of fraternal charity.

One final note on the concept of the Church as communion; it is something given from above. In its document on the Church, the Second Vatican Council quotes St. Cyprian who said that the Church is "a people brought into unity [communion] from the unity of the Father, the Son and the Holy Spirit." And just prior to that, the Council refers to the Holy Spirit as the one who unifies the Church in communion and in the works of ministry. What this means is that we must first think of Christian communion and fellowship in a vertical relationship to the Blessed Trinity, as the source and the model, and only then can we effectively construct the Christian community along horizontal lines.

From what we have seen thus far, a question arises as regards membership in the People of God and the fellowship or communion of believers. If all validly baptized persons are members of the People of God, are they all members of the Catholic Church? There is valid baptism outside the Roman Catholic Church, because if anyone administers that sacrament with the intention of doing what Christ commanded, baptizing with water and the proper formula, the effects of baptism take place. Consequently, that individual is a member, not necessarily of the visible Catholic Church, but a member of the Church of Christ. In its document on the Church, the Second Vatican Council states it this way:

> This is the sole Church of Christ which in the Creed we profess to be one, holy, catholic, and apostolic. . . . This Church, constituted and organized as a society in the present world, subsists in the Catholic Church, which is governed by the successor of Peter and by the bishops in communion with him. Nevertheless, many elements of sanctification and of truth are found outside its visible confines. Since these are gifts belonging to the Church of Christ, they are forces impelling towards Catholic unity. (LG 8)

The *Decree on Ecumenism* is even more explicit, saying that those who "believe in Christ and have been properly baptized are put in some, though imperfect, communion with the Catholic Church. . . . But even in spite of obstacles it remains true that all who have been justified by faith in baptism are incorporated into Christ; they therefore have a right to be called Christians, and with good reason are accepted as brothers by the children of the Catholic Church" (UR 2). Therefore, all those outside the Catholic Church who have been validly baptized in water and the Holy Spirit, as Christ commanded, are members of the Church of Christ.

And what is required for full membership in the Catholic Church? Any church, to be a church, should have a basic unity among its members; it should in some sense be a communion, namely, a grouping of like-minded persons. Therefore the first requisite is unity of faith. All the members of a church should accept the same religious truths, both doctrinal and moral. And where does one find these religious truths? Throughout the centuries the members of the Church have professed the one and the same faith in the recitation of the Creeds, from the Apostles' Creed down to the Credo of the People of God, promulgated by Pope Paul VI in 1968. Each Sunday and feastday throughout the liturgical year the People of God profess their faith by reciting the Nicene Creed at Mass.

The second requisite for full membership in the Catholic Church is the reception of the sacraments. We believe that Jesus Christ instituted the seven sacraments as visible signs and channels of the graces we need throughout our lifetime, from baptism to the last anointing. It is no accident that the first document completed by the Second Vatican Council was the Constitution on the Sacred Liturgy. And Pope Paul VI stated that the liturgy is also first "in intrinsic worth and in importance for the life of the Church." The document itself asserts that "the liturgy is the summit toward which the activity is directed. . . . For the goal of apostolic endeavor is that all who are made sons of God by faith and baptism should come together to praise God in the midst of his Church, to take part in the Sacrifice and to eat the Lord's Supper" (SC 10). Indeed, the liturgy is our faith in action and celebration. In addition to that, the document on the liturgy states that "it is through the liturgy especially that the faithful are enabled to express in their lives and manifest to others the mystery of Christ and the real nature of the true Church" (SC 2). Hence the witness value of participation in the sacred liturgy and the worthy reception of the sacraments.

The third requirement for full membership in the Catholic Church is obedience to ecclesiastical authority as exercised by the Pope and all bishops in union with him. In the revised *Code of Canon Law* we read that full communion with the Catholic Church is effected through "the bonds of profession of faith, the sacraments, and ecclesiastical governance" (can. 205). In its *Decree on the Pastoral Office of Bishops*, the Second Vatican Council declared that the Holy Father "has been granted by God supreme, full, immediate and universal power in the care of souls. . . . He is therefore endowed with the primacy of ordinary power over all the churches" (CD 2). The bishops throughout the world "take the place of the apostles as pastors of souls and, together with the Supreme Pontiff and subject to his authority, they are commissioned to perpetuate the work of Christ, the eternal Pastor" (CD 2). It is worth noting that, according to the Second Vatican Council, the primary duty of the bishop as head of the local church or diocese is the ministry of the word, both as preacher and as teacher. The members of the local church, on the other hand, are urged to be loyal to their bishop and to "be formed by him into one community in the Holy Spirit through the Gospel and the Eucharist" (CD 11).

Having discussed the meaning of the term "People of God," and its various ramifications, we should have a clearer concept of the Church as mystery and communion. We should likewise have an appreciation for the basic equality of all the members of the Church on the basis of their baptism into Christ through water and the Holy Spirit. We are now in a position to look at the Church more closely and to focus our attention on the various classes that make up the People of God. To do this, we have selected another term that describes the Church: the Mystical Body of Christ. To speak of the Church exclusively as the People of God could readily give the impression that the Church is nothing more than a conglomerate assembly of people without names or faces. But God has called each one of us by name; indeed, however important it is to see the Church as community, it is equally important to consider the individuals who make up the community of the Church.

THE MYSTICAL BODY OF CHRIST

The description of the Church as the Mystical Body of Christ became a household word under Pope Pius XII but its use actually goes back to St. Paul. This great Apostle to the Gentiles was especially aware of the manifold gifts that God bestows on his Church and the variety of charisms and ministries allotted to individual members of the People of God. His teaching prevents us from exaggerating the term ''People of God'' to such an extent that we reduce all the members of the Church to an undifferentiated conglomerate.

> Just as each of us has one body with many members, and not all the members have the same function, so too we, though many, are one body in Christ and individually members of one another. We have gifts that differ according to the favor bestowed on each of us. One's gift may be prophecy; its use should be in proportion to his faith. It may be the gift of ministry; it should be used for service. One who is a teacher should use his gift for teaching; one with the power of exhortation should exhort. He who gives alms should do so generously; he who rules should exercise his authority with care; he who performs works of mercy should do so cheerfully (Rm 12:4-8).

Pope Pius XII gave the Church the same teaching in his Encyclical *Mystici Corporis*. It is somewhat of a surprise that the Second Vatican Council had so little to say about the Church as the Mystical Body of Christ. Does this mean that the document *Lumen Gentium* has superseded the Encyclical of Pope Pius XII? Does it at least put the two terms, ''People of God'' and ''Mystical Body of Christ'', in opposition to one another? The answer to both of these

questions is in the negative. The fact is that Pope Pius XII gave the
Church a beautiful summary of biblical, theological and pastoral
testimony to the Church as the Mystical Body of Christ, but he did
not ignore completely the common unity of the faithful. It is worth
citing one of the key statements that is pertinent to our topic:

> If we would define and describe this true Church of Jesus Christ
> — which is the one, holy, catholic, apostolic, Roman Church —
> we shall find nothing more noble, more sublime, or more divine
> than the expression 'the Mystical Body of Jesus Christ,' an
> expression that springs from and is, as it were, the fair flowering
> of the repeated teaching of the Sacred Scriptures and the holy
> Fathers. . . . When the Fathers of the Church sing the praises of
> this Mystical Body of Christ, . . . they are thinking not only of
> those who have received holy orders, but of all those who,
> following the evangelical counsels, pass their lives either ac-
> tively among men or hidden in the silence of the cloister or who
> aim at combining the active and contemplative life according to
> their institutes; as also of those who, though living in the world,
> consecrate themselves wholeheartedly to spiritual and corporal
> works of mercy, and of those who live in the state of holy
> matrimony. Indeed, let this be clearly understood, especially in
> these our days; fathers and mothers of families, those who are
> godparents through baptism, and in particular those members of
> the laity who collaborate with the ecclesiastical hierarchy in
> spreading the kingdom of the divine Redeemer, occupy an
> honorable, if often a lowly, place in the Christian community,
> and even they, under the impulse of God and with his help, can
> reach the heights of supreme holiness which, Jesus Christ has
> promised, will never be wanting to the Church.

It is evident from the foregoing passage that Pope Pius
XII was discussing the Roman Catholic Church and the three
conditions required for full membership: faith in the teaching
of the Church, reception of the sacraments, and obedience to

ecclesiastical authority. He did not, however, as did the Second Vatican Council, take up the wider question of membership in the Church of Christ, which is effected through valid baptism and therefore includes Christians outside the Roman Catholic Church. The Encyclical treats of problems within the Catholic Church, and in those terms Pope Pius XII could say that the Mystical Body of Christ *is* the one, holy, catholic, and apostolic Church of Rome. The Second Vatican Council, on the other hand, uses a more ecumenical approach and therefore, after admitting membership of all baptized Christians in the Church of Christ, it states that the Church of Christ *subsists* in the Catholic Church.

We can leave it to the theologians and canonists to argue over the possible differences and relative merits of those two documents. What is important for our purposes is to see that the term "Mystical Body of Christ" refers to all who, through baptism, are members of that body of which Christ is the Head. And since it is a body with various members and functions, all the members share in that life which comes from Christ, but in greater or lesser degree. Secondly, as a member of the Mystical Body, each Christian has a specific function to perform in the Church; consequently, there is a variety of ministries in the Church, but all aim at the same goal, namely to extend the kingdom of God on earth. St. Paul expresses this doctrine clearly and emphatically:

> The body is one and has many members, but all the members, many though they are, are one body; and so it is with Christ. . . . If the foot should say, "Because I am not a hand I do not belong to the body," would it then no longer belong to the body? If the ear should say, "Because I am not an eye I do not belong to the body," would it then no longer belong to the body? If the body were all eye, what would happen to our hearing? If it were all ear, what would happen to our smelling? As it is, God has set each member of the body in the place he wanted it to be. If all the members were alike, where would the body be? There are indeed

> many different members, but one body. The eye cannot say to
> the hand, ''I do not need you,'' any more than the head can say to
> the feet, ''I do not need you.'' Even those members of the body
> which seem less important are in fact indispensable. (I Cor
> 12:12-22)

It has been said, and rightly so, that in the Church there is
unity of mission and diversity of ministries. It has also been said
that what we want in the Church is unity without uniformity and
pluralism without division. These two statements serve very well
as signposts that point the way to achieving a proper balance
between the equality of all the People of God and the differences
among the members of the Mystical Body of Christ. Pope John
Paul II touched on this matter in his talk at the opening of the Synod
on the Laity in 1987:

> The Church is the Body in which Christ's life flows into the
> faithful who unite themselves to him in a mysterious and real
> way through the sacraments. She is at the same time a People,
> the new People of God, which has Christ as its Head, the dignity
> and freedom of the sons of God as its condition, the new precept
> of love as its law, and the Kingdom of God as its end.

If it is by reason of their baptism that there is a basic equality
among all the members of the Church and a proportional sharing in
the mission of the Church, there must be something in addition to
baptism that accounts for the diversity of functions and ministries.
In the beginning, according to the teaching of St. Paul, one's
service or function in the Church was determined by the gift or
charism received from the Holy Spirit, as we saw in the quotation
from the Letter to the Romans. The gifts differ, says St. Paul,
according to the favor bestowed on each one. But by the end of the
first century, as the Church necessarily became more structured,
greater emphasis was placed on the leadership of bishops, and in

time it was the ecclesiastical authority that allocated the various functions and ministries. More and more the ordinary baptized Christians were dependent on the clergy for services rendered; and more and more the concept of "ministry" was related to the ministry of the word (preaching and teaching) and the ministry of the Eucharist. Even in modern times all ministries and approved apostolates are for the most part controlled by ecclesiastical authority.

There is yet another, rather general, reason for the diversity of functions and ministries in the Church, due in large part to the way in which the Church has developed through the centuries. With the reception of holy orders certain baptized Christians enter the ranks of the clergy and dedicate themselves to the priestly ministry; other baptized Christians may commit themselves to a life of poverty, chastity and obedience in an institute of the consecrated life; still others — the majority — will receive the sacrament of matrimony and dedicate themselves to the apostolate of the "domestic" church which is the family. In each case the individuals are something more than baptized Christians. Something has been added, and it serves as the basis for placing them in a distinctive state of life. For all practical purposes, therefore, there are various classes of Christians, each with duties proper to their state of life: the clergy, the persons in the consecrated life, and the married or unmarried laity. Beneath that, of course, there are the various professions, trades and careers, and they also offer distinct opportunities for Christians to extend the kingdom of God and spread the Gospel message. We shall have more to say about this when we treat of ministry in a later chapter.

We have referred to the statement that the Church needs unity without uniformity and pluralism without division. This is desirable in any society but it is not always easy to achieve. Many of the older generation, habituated to a pre-Vatican II Church, find it very difficult to accept some of the changes introduced by the Second Vatican Council. The younger generation, who never knew the "old" Church, are faced with a much greater challenge, however. They are the ones who will shoulder the responsibility for carrying on the mission of the Church in the future.

THE MISSION OF THE CHURCH

Every member of the Church is called and every member of the Church is sent. Consequently, the Second Vatican Council states in its document on the laity: "The Christian vocation is, of its nature, a vocation to the apostolate as well" (AA 2). Within the diversity of ministries, all have an active part to play in the single mission of the Church. Indeed, the Church "is by its very nature missionary," as the Fathers of Vatican II say in their *Decree on the Missionary Activity of the Church*. We read later in the same document: "As members of the living Christ, incorporated into him and made like him by baptism, confirmation and the Eucharist, all the faithful have an obligation to collaborate in the expansion and spread of his Body, so that they might bring it to fullness as soon as possible (cf. Ep 4:13)" (AG 36).

Christ instituted his Church with a specific mission, which is described as follows by the Second Vatican Council in its document on the laity: "to spread the kingdom of Christ over all the earth for the glory of God the Father, to make all men partakers in redemption and salvation, and through them to establish the right relationship of the entire world to Christ" (AA 2).

There are numerous implications in the foregoing statement. First of all, we should note that the Church of Christ truly is Christ's Church; it is of divine, not human, origin. "The mystery of the holy Church is already brought to light in the way it was founded. For the Lord Jesus inaugurated his Church by preaching the Good News, that is, the coming of the kingdom of God" (LG 5). The Church is therefore the "sacrament" of Christ, the instrument through which he continues his salvific work throughout the centuries.

Secondly — and it bears repeating — the mission of the Church is not restricted to the ministry of the hierarchy; not any more than the definition of the Church applies only to the hierarchy. As we have just seen, the mission of the Church pertains to all the members of the Church because all are called and all are sent. It is true, of course, that the hierarchy have a particular, well-defined role in the Church's mission, but the Second Vatican Council also called for closer collaboration between the hierarchy and the laity.

Thirdly, the mission of the Church is eminently spiritual: to bring Christ's redeeming grace to all nations and to bring the entire world into relationship with him. Christ himself provided the means by which this mission is to be carried out, namely, through the preaching of the Gospel, the administration of the sacraments, and the formation of an ecclesial community. In our times, more than ever before, all the members of the Church are invited and urged to perform the particular function that falls to their lot, according to their state and condition of life.

Finally, the Church does not exist for itself, but for others. Whatever the Church has — the Gospel message, the sacraments, infallible teaching authority, priesthood, charisms and holiness — it has from above, through the merits of Jesus Christ and the power of the Holy Spirit. The mission of the Church is ministry or service to others and not self-preservation. And the members of the Church, especially the hierarchy, must take care not to cultivate a mentality similar to that of foreign diplomats serving their country. Rather, the focus of their attention should be on the people they serve in the local church.

A final word is in order concerning the mission of the Church. It has a double aspect, the first of which is obviously the extension of the kingdom of God throughout the world so that all nations may be brought into a relationship with Christ. That was the command of Christ to the apostles, to preach the Gospel to every nation. The Church is in the world, therefore, to act as a leaven to renew the face of the earth. And when we think of this aspect of the Church's mission, we logically stress the external activities of the Church: to teach, to sanctify and to govern the Christian community.

There is a second aspect of the mission of the Church which is more internal and more personal: to bring men and women to a share in Christ's saving redemption. Christ commanded all his followers to be perfect as the heavenly Father is perfect. Therefore the mission of the Church to the world must eventually touch the lives of individual Christians and inspire them to strive for the perfection of the Christian life. And as the numbers of such Christians increase, the example of their Christian witness will be much more effective in promoting the mission of the Church than can be achieved by words or actions. A modern theologian, Father John G. Arintero, O.P., has developed these sentiments in a masterly fashion in his work, *The Mystical Evolution*, as is evident from the following passage:

> Without an exposition, however brief, of the basis of the spiritual life and the growth in Christian perfection, the defense of our religion would always be incomplete and defective. To make God's Church loved, no better way can be found than to show the ineffable attractions of its inner life. To present only its inflexible exterior aspect is almost to disfigure it and make it disagreeable; it is, in a sense, to despoil it of its glory and its principal enchantments. All its glory is from within. . . .
>
> Presented as it is in itself, without disguise or mitigation, and without weakening and disfigurement through the abject and narrow standards of human evaluation, the Church, full of grace and truth in imitation of its Spouse, gives perpetual testimony of its divine mission and is its own best defense. Actually, divine truth needs no defense; it needs only to be presented in its innate splendor and irresistible force. (Vol. I, Introduction, p. 11)

CHAPTER 2

THE FAITHFUL OF CHRIST

After considering the Church as the People of God and the Mystical Body of Christ, we now focus our attention more closely on the members of the Church. The shifting of our attention is similar to what happens when the television camera first surveys the entire crowd in a stadium, and then zooms in to highlight the various groups or individuals in the crowd. And since there is a difference of perspective from seeing the Church as the People of God or the Mystical Body of Christ, there is also another term to designate this difference. The *Code of Canon Law* uses the Latin term "*Christifideles*," which is translated as "Christ's faithful" or "the faithful of Christ."

Formerly the expression "the faithful" referred only to the laity, but now it is used to include each and every member of the Church, as is the term "the People of God." As in the latter case, we have returned to the original meaning of the word "faithful." Consequently, what we have said about the fundamental equality of all the People of God and the obligation to share in the mission of the Church is likewise applicable when we speak of Christ's faithful. And the common obligation to participate in the Church's mission means that all the faithful are called to strive for personal holiness or the perfection of charity; they are obliged, according to their competence and condition of life, to strengthen the faith of those who are Christians and to attract to the faith those who are not; and they are to strive to imbue the temporal order with Christian values.

Of course, as we have already seen, while there is a fundamental equality among all the faithful, there is likewise a distinction of functions and ministries. But whenever the Second Vatican Council referred to that which is common to all baptized Christians, it used one or another of the following words: "the baptized," "believers," "members", "Christians", "the faithful of Christ", or simply "the faithful." The 1983 *Code of Canon Law*, however, treats of all the various groupings in the Church under the title "The People of God," and then, when enumerating the rights and duties of both the clergy and the laity, it uses the heading "Christ's faithful." Therefore, membership in the People of God should be expressed by the term "Christ's faithful" or "the faithful of Christ," which name applies to all baptized Christians, whether clergy, consecrated persons or laity. The definition of "Christ's faithful" is found in canon 204:

> The Christian faithful are those who, inasmuch as they have been incorporated in Christ through baptism, have been constituted as the People of God; for this reason, since they have become sharers in Christ's priestly, prophetic and royal office in their own manner, they are called to exercise the mission which God has entrusted to the Church to fulfill in the world, in accord with the condition proper to each one.

Later, in canon 208, we read: "In virtue of their rebirth in Christ, there exists among all the Christian faithful a true equality with regard to dignity and the activity whereby all cooperate in the building up of the Body of Christ in accord with each one's own condition and function." This same idea was expressed by Pope John Paul II in his address to the Bishops' Synod of 1987: "All lay people have a dignity that they hold in common with clerics and religious, since there is only one people brought into unity from the unity of the Father, the Son and the Holy Spirit. . . . Whoever receives baptism, confirmation and the Eucharist commits himself or herself to follow Christ and to witness to him with his or her whole life.''

Every member of Christ's faithful, therefore, has a legal status in the Church by reason of the sacrament of baptism, which incorporates the individual as a member of the People of God. Thus, canon 96 states that ''by baptism one is incorporated into the Church of Christ and is constituted a person in it, with duties and rights which are proper to Christians, in keeping with their condition.''

The bond that unites the People of God as a social group is the sacrament of baptism. Those who are reborn through water and the Holy Spirit, though they previously had no relation to one another except their common humanity, are now ''a chosen race, a royal priesthood, a holy nation, a people he claims for his own. . . . Once you were not a people, but now you are God's people'' (1 P 2:9-10). From this new relationship with one another as baptized Christians, with a responsibility for promoting the mission of Christ's Church, flows their status as individual persons in the Church, with specific rights and duties according to their condition and state of life. Similarly, a person born in a given nation is a citizen of that nation and is endowed with all the rights and duties according to the laws of that nation. However, it is important to bear in mind that in the Church, as in a nation, the manner of exercising one's rights and performing one's duties will differ from one person to another. Thus, in the Church the listing of the rights and duties of the clergy or those in the consecrated life will differ greatly from those pertaining to the laity.

Moreover, although all baptized Christians are incorporated into Christ, there are varying degrees of that incorporation. Some Christians lead fervent lives and constantly grow in holiness; others may be in the state of grace but are lukewarm Christians; and finally there are some who, because of their state of serious sin, are dead branches on the vine that is Christ. Yet, as long as they have received valid baptism, they are members of the People of God. In like manner, some citizens of a nation are good and loyal citizens, while others are criminals, but the latter do not lose their citizenship because of their crimes.

From a canonical or legal point of view there are also degrees of incorporation in Christ's Church. We have previously made a distinction between membership in the "Church of Christ" and in the Catholic Church. All validly baptized Christians, whatever their religious affiliation, are members of the Church of Christ. But since the Second Vatican Council declared that the Church of Christ subsists or is found in its totality in the Roman Catholic Church, something more than baptism is required for complete and full membership in the Church of Christ. That is the basis for the declaration we find in the Vatican II document on the Church:

> Fully incorporated into the Church are those who, possessing the Spirit of Christ, accept all the means of salvation given to the Church together with her entire organization, and who — by the bonds constituted by the profession of faith, the sacraments, ecclesiastical government, and communion — are joined in the visible structure of the Church of Christ, who rules her through the Supreme Pontiff and the bishops. Even though incorporated into the Church, one who does not however persevere in charity is not saved. He remains indeed in the bosom of the Church, but "in body" not "in heart." (LG 14)

Canon 205 likewise states that full communion with the Church requires union with Christ in his visible body through the bonds of "profession of faith, the sacraments and ecclesiastical governance." But the members of the Church cannot be purely passive recipients of the sacraments who are obedient to ecclesiastical authority. Since they share in the priestly, prophetic and priestly functions of Christ, they are called upon to exercise these same functions according to their condition and state of life. This applies to the laity as well as the clergy, as is stated in the document of Vatican Council II on the laity:

> In the Church there is a diversity of ministry but unity of mission. To the apostles and their successors Christ has entrusted the office of teaching, sanctifying and governing in his name and by his power. But the laity are made to share in the priestly, prophetic and kingly office of Christ; they have therefore in the Church and in the world their own assignment in the mission of the whole People of God. (AA 2)

We can see from the foregoing quotations that the priestly, prophetic and kingly functions of Christ as shared by the faithful are exercised in the Church under three titles: the sanctifying mission of the Church (the priestly function), the teaching mission of the Church (the prophetic function), and ecclesiastical government (the kingly function). However, both the Council documents and the *Code of Canon Law* constantly add the phrases "according to their condition" or "in their own manner." What this means is that although all the faithful of Christ share in the priestly, prophetic and kingly functions of Christ by sanctifying, teaching and governing, they do not all perform those functions to the same degree. This necessarily calls for a diversity of ministries as well as a differentiation of classes or groups of the members of the Church. Moreover, not all of the faithful will have the same rights and duties in the Church.

CLERGY, CONSECRATED PERSONS AND LAITY

> By divine institution, among Christ's faithful there are in the Church sacred ministers, who in law are also called clerics; the others are called lay people.

> Drawn from both groups are those of Christ's faithful who,
> professing the evangelical counsels through vows or other sacred
> bonds recognized and approved by the Church, are consecrated
> to God in their own special way and promote the saving mission
> of the Church. Their state, although it does not belong to the
> hierarchical structure of the Church, does pertain to its life and
> holiness.

Thus does canon 207 describe the three fundamental classes of the faithful of Christ or, if you wish, three basic states of the Christian life. It is worth noting also that only two of these classes of the faithful — the clergy and the laity — were instituted by Christ. Does this mean that the life of the evangelical counsels, as lived by consecrated persons, is not of divine origin but is a purely human creation? You will find defenders of both positions, but a middle course would seem to be that, while Christ did not explicitly establish a third class of the faithful, the consecrated life is certainly of divine origin. First of all, because Christ gave as the first and greatest commandment: "Thou shalt love the Lord thy God with thy whole heart, with all thy soul, and with all thy mind" (Mt 22:37); and anyone who reaches a high degree of the perfection of charity will also live the evangelical counsels according to his or her state of life. Secondly, we can trace the consecrated life back to Christ because he himself lived poverty, chastity and obedience, although he did not institute the consecrated life as a specific state of life or class of Christians. Indeed, all the faithful of Christ are called to the perfection of charity, and that is why the foregoing canon rightly asserts that the evangelical counsels can be practiced by both clergy and laity. But as a distinct way of life approved by the Church, that came into existence much later.

It is of interest to note that the eminent theologian Hans Urs von Balthasar, in his book *The Christian State of Life*, maintains that the apostles lived the evangelical counsels — at least the counsels of poverty and obedience — as soon as they were called by Christ to follow him. He says that "the Twelve were separated from the multitude for a qualitatively higher mission. They were not to return home. . . . They were no longer to think of themselves, but were to proclaim the nearness of the kingdom of heaven. . . . They were to renounce themselves in order to identify themselves with the mind and mission of him who sent them." He then concludes that "the state of the evangelical counsels existed before the priestly state" (p. 172).

Responding to the invitation of Christ, the apostles left all things and followed him, and in making a total commitment to Christ they embarked on the life of the evangelical counsels. There is, however, a special problem as regards the counsel of continence or chastity, since we know that St. Peter, at least, was a married man. The problem is readily resolved if we realize that any lay person can observe the evangelical counsels, but would do so according to his or her state of life, which is quite different from the state of life proper to consecrated persons. Hans Urs von Balthasar responds to the question as follows:

> [Christ] required this total renunciation not only of his apostles, but also of all those who wanted to give themselves entirely to him, to follow him wherever he went (cf. Mt 8:19) — including then, certainly, those not called to the priesthood. But he required it a fortiori of his priests. Their renunciation of the world is consistently depicted as "leaving all things," that is, as complete poverty, and as "following the Lord wherever he went," that is, as perfect obedience. But the Lord, as we have seen, did not insist on virginity, no doubt because the apostles, whose roots were in the Old Testament, were for the most part already married and "what . . . God has joined together, let no man put asunder" (Mt 19:6). It is here that the first difference between the priesthood and the state of the counsels makes its appearance in the Gospels: the state of the counsels requires virginity in addition to the poverty and obedience required of the

priesthood. If Peter, who was married, appears as the representa-
tive of the official priesthood, the virgin apostles John and Paul
are the designated representatives of that personal and interior
priesthood that is the explicit following of the High Priest "who
offered himself unblemished unto God" (Heb 9:14). (p. 281.)

It has been traditional in theology to state that bishops and
religious are in the "state of perfection," but what does this mean?
St. Thomas Aquinas treated of this question at great length in his
Summa Theologiae (IIa IIae, qq. 183-189) and it is worthwhile to
summarize his teaching. After demonstrating that Christian perfection consists primarily in the virtue of charity, and that all Christians are called to the perfection of charity, St. Thomas teaches that
anyone who attains to the perfection of charity will practice the
evangelical counsels according to his or her state of life. But the
expression "state of perfection" is a technical term; it applies to
bishops, says St. Thomas, because they "oblige themselves to
those things which pertain to perfection by accepting the pastoral
charge," and it applies to religious because they "bind themselves
by vow to abstain from worldly things, in order to dedicate
themselves more freely to God." But St. Thomas likewise states
that "nothing prevents some from being perfect who are not in the
state of perfection and others from being in the state of perfection
who are not perfect."

Christ, therefore, called certain individuals out of the
multitude to be his priests, and he conferred on them the power and
authority to minister to God's People in his name. It is not necessary to prove the divine institution of the priesthood in the Church;
the testimony of the Gospels and Epistles is ample proof. It is
likewise evident that although all the baptized faithful share in the
priesthood of Christ, there is an essential difference between the
priesthood of the laity and the ordained, ministerial priesthood. But
what may raise questions is the fact that Pope Paul VI made radical
changes regarding ministers and ministries in the Church when he

issued the document *Ministeria Quaedam* in 1972. Traditionally a young man entered the clerical state with the reception of the tonsure; then he advanced to the priesthood through a series of what were called "minor orders," subdiaconate and diaconate. With the new legislation, however, the only so-called minor orders that remain are lector and acolyte; the subdiaconate has been abolished in the Latin Church; and a layman, single or married, may present himself for ordination as a deacon, at which time he enters the clerical state.

If, now, someone has a problem with the fact that Pope Paul VI abolished the minor orders as clerical ministries and made them lay ministries, that he suppressed the subdiaconate, and that he permitted laymen to become permanent deacons, the answer is that all of these offices and ministries are of ecclesiastical, and therefore human, origin. If they had been instituted by Christ, no ecclesiastical official would have the authority to change them. But what the Church has created, the Church can adapt or abolish.

What is important for our purposes is to recognize that the faithful of Christ, members of the People of God, are divided into three classes: those who have received holy orders, those who have embraced the consecrated life of the evangelical counsels, and those who constitute the largest group in the Church, the laity. The Second Vatican Council treated of each of these groups in particular and gave to the universal Church documents that serve as valuable guidelines for the adaptation and renewal of the local churches. But since the term "faithful of Christ" applies equally to all the members of the Church, and each individual is constituted a person in the Church, with certain rights and duties, we now turn to the *Code of Canon Law*, where we find a listing of the rights and obligations that are shared by every Catholic without distinction of persons.

RIGHTS OF THE CHRISTIAN FAITHFUL

When he officially promulgated the *Code of Canon Law* in January, 1983, Pope John Paul II stated that among the elements that express the true and authentic image of the Church are the following: the teaching on the Church as the People of God; hierarchical authority as a service to the People of God; the Church as communion; the relationship between the local church and the universal Church and between collegiality and primacy. He then referred to ''the teaching according to which all the members of the People of God share, each in his or her own measure, in the threefold priestly, prophetic and kingly office of Christ, with which teaching is associated also that which looks to the duties and rights of Christ's faithful, and specifically the laity.''

Before treating in particular of the various classes of the faithful of Christ, the *Code of Canon Law* has an introductory section that lists the rights and duties that are common to all the members of the Church. Logically, the first note that is struck is that of equality, as we read in canon 208: ''Flowing from their rebirth in Christ through baptism, there is a genuine equality of dignity and action among all of Christ's faithful. Because of this equality they all contribute, each according to his or her own condition or office, to the building up of the Body of Christ.'' Since all the members of the Church are equal, whatever is stated in canons 208 to 223 applies to every Catholic, regardless of his or her condition or state in life. We have had occasion to speak of this equality in the Church numerous times and the reason is that it is a concept that is constantly recurring in the documents of Vatican Council II and in the *Code of Canon Law*.

It would be well to note at the outset that when we speak of equal rights, the term ''rights'' can be understood in various ways. Some rights are so fundamental that they precede any law and are in fact the basis on which good laws are formulated; for example, the inalienable human rights. Then there are some rights that pertain to a person's freedom of choice; for example, to use a given right or to forego it, whether it be a right to act or a right to receive. Finally, some rights may be so closely related to the common good of a society that a person should normally exercise that right; for example, the right to participate in the mission of the Church according to one's capability.

The exercise of rights in any society should always be regulated — and sometimes curtailed — in view of the common good of that society. And by "common good" we do not mean what the majority want, for it could happen that what the majority want would be detrimental of the society as a whole. The common good of any society is determined by the goal or purpose for which that society was instituted. Consequently, a society should be made up of members who are seeking the same goal and are willing to work together to achieve that goal.

Another determining factor of the exercise of one's rights has to do with the circumstances which may have some bearing on the individual case. Thus, the citizen in a democracy has the right to vote, but only after attaining the legal age; an individual has a right to earn a living, but not necessarily in this or that profession; and a Catholic has the right to take an active part in the liturgy, but not to usurp the functions proper to the clergy. For that reason, the laws of the Church, when treating of rights and duties of the faithful, frequently add the qualifying clause: "according to one's condition and state of life."

Coming now to the various rights of the Christian faithful, we want to begin by emphasizing once more that these are rights that are shared by all the different classes of the faithful of Christ, be they clergy, laity or consecrated persons. Some of the rights will imply a corresponding duty; for example, if the laity have a right to receive the sacraments, then the clergy have an obligation to perform that ministry. Finally, we shall follow closely the legislation of the Church as given in the *Code of Canon Law*, although we

shall not necessarily follow the numerical order of the canons. And
for those familiar with the various documents of the Second Vatican Council, they cannot fail to notice how closely — sometimes
literally — some of the canons repeat the teaching of Vatican
Council II. That is to be expected, of course, since the documents
of Vatican Council II are the directives for the future of the Church.

> *CANON 214*:   Christ's faithful have the right to worship God
> according to the provisions of their own rite approved by the
> lawful Pastors of the Church; they also have the right to follow
> their own form of spiritual life, provided it is in accord with
> Church teaching.

By baptism each Christian belongs to a particular rite, each of
which has its own liturgy and its own hierarchy. Before the large
waves of emigration took place in the nineteenth century, the one
Catholic Church was composed of the Latin Church in the West
and the various uniate Churches in the East. They all accepted the
Holy Father in Rome as the successor of St. Peter and the Vicar of
Christ, but the Eastern Churches differed even among themselves
as regards liturgy, language and hierarchy. In the present century
the Churches of the East and the West have moved much closer
together, both physically and psychologically. It is not at all
unusual, especially in the large urban centers, to encounter members of the Greek, Ukrainian or Maronite rites, for example. And
although they would normally worship in their own churches
according to their own liturgy and receive the sacraments from
their own clergy, the present law of the Church allows them to
receive the sacraments of penance, Eucharist and anointing of the
sick from priests of a different rite. Canon 844 even allows a
Catholic priest to give those same sacraments to members of the
Eastern Churches not in union with Rome, if they request them and
are properly disposed, and also to members of other Churches that
the Holy See approves. The same canon states that when it is

physically or morally impossible for Catholics to receive any of those same three sacraments from their own priest, they may receive them from a minister of a Church in which those sacraments are valid.

Given the greater freedom as regards the reception of the sacraments, which are channels of grace and means of sanctification, it is not surprising that this same canon speaks of the spiritual life of the faithful. In its document on the Church the Second Vatican Council stated that all Christians, regardless of their condition or state of life, are called to the perfection of charity. And while it is true that there is only one perfection — the perfection of charity — there are many ways in which the love that is charity can be experienced and manifested. These different ways are what constitute the variety of spiritualities in the Church. In ancient times the classification was neat and simple; it was a question of either the active or the contemplative life, and theologians such as St. Augustine, St. Gregory the Great and St. Thomas Aquinas used the examples of Martha and Mary to explain the difference. And yet, even for Martha and Mary, what made them saints was not what they did, so much as the love with which they did it. We shall treat of this subject in greater detail later on, but for the present it suffices to say that this canon 214 demonstrates that the Church does recognize a variety of paths to the perfection of charity and defends the right of each Christian to follow his or her form of the spiritual life. And if anyone contends that there is only one form or school of spirituality for everyone, we need only point to the marvelous variety and diversity among the saints of the Church, each of whom attained to heroic virtue and the perfection of charity. As a further protection of the freedom of the faithful in this matter, canon 219 states: "All Christ's faithful have the right to immunity from any kind of coercion in choosing a state of life."

> *CANON 213*:   Christ's faithful have the right to be assisted by their Pastors from the spiritual riches of the Church, especially by the word of God and the sacraments.

Previously, canon 212, #2, stated that the faithful have the right to make known their needs, especially their spiritual needs, to the Pastors of the Church. There is, therefore, a corresponding duty on the part of the clergy, who are ordained for ministry, to instruct the faithful through preaching and to be available for the administration of the sacraments. In fact, canon 843 reminds the clergy that they "may not deny the sacraments to those who opportunely ask for them, are properly disposed and are not prohibited by law from receiving them."

> *CANON 212, #3*:   [Christ's faithful] have the right, indeed at times the duty, in keeping with their knowledge, competence and position, to manifest to their sacred Pastors their views on matters which concern the good of the Church. They have the right also to make their views known to others of Christ's faithful, but in doing so they must always respect the integrity of faith and morals, show due reverence to the Pastors, and take into account both the common good and the dignity of individuals.

The two preceding canons are taken almost literally from paragraph 37 of the *Dogmatic Constitution on the Church*, issued by the Second Vatican Council and it is worthwhile to note the similarity:

> Like all Christians, the laity have the right to receive in abundance the help of the spiritual goods of the Church, especially that of the word of God and the sacraments, from the pastors. To the latter the laity should disclose their needs and desires with that liberty and confidence which befits children of God and brothers of Christ. By reason of the knowledge, competence or pre-eminence which they have, the laity are empowered — indeed sometimes obliged — to manifest their opinion on those things which pertain to the good of the Church. If the occasion should

arise, this should be done through the institutions established by the Church for that purpose, and always with truth, courage, and prudence, and with reverence and charity towards those who, by reason of their office, represent the person of Christ. (LG 37).

We have here an example of a right that is qualified by certain restrictions. Since the exercise of the right to express one's views and opinions may sometimes take the form of criticism or complaint against another person or group, charity and justice should prevail at all times. Canon 220 states: "No one may unlawfully harm the good reputation which a person enjoys, or violate the right of every person to protect his or her privacy." One can avoid harming another person's good name or working out of purely selfish motives if he or she follows the procedure outlined above. Is this particular matter for the good of the diocese or parish? Is my position in accord with the Church's teaching on faith and morals as well as the ecclesiastical laws? Am I competent to express these views or promote this suggestion? Is there a proper channel in the Church through which I should operate?

CANON 215: Christ's faithful may freely establish and direct associations which serve charitable or pious purposes or which foster the Christian vocation in the world, and they may hold meetings to pursue these purposes by common effort.

CANON 216: Since they share the Church's mission, all Christ's faithful have the right to promote and support apostolic action, by their own initiative, undertaken according to their state and condition. No initiative, however, can lay claim to the title "Catholic" without the consent of the competent ecclesiastical authority.

We have here what we could call the ''right of assembly'' that is enjoyed by all the members of the Church. These two canons, however, would seem to apply especially to the laity, since the clergy and the members of the consecrated life are not allowed to join associations that are incompatible with their duties or state in life. It should be noted, however, that although they are members of the clergy, permanent deacons are not restricted as regards the use of this right; for example, they may hold public office, join labor unions, and engage in business (cf. canon 288). Nevertheless, as stated, the canon allows any of Christ's faithful to establish, join, or direct associations and societies that are founded for charitable or religious purposes. Later, canon 298 lists some of the aims of associations of Christ's faithful: to foster a more perfect life; to promote public worship or Christian teaching; initiatives for evangelization, works of piety or charity, and those which animate the temporal order with the Christian spirit. Then, there is a very lengthy and detailed treatment of the various types of associations, extending from canon 299 to canon 329.

For those familiar with the former laws of the Church, which stressed the role of ecclesiastical authority in establishing or approving various types of associations, the present legislation represents a welcome change. Now the initiative to found or govern certain types of associations can come from the people themselves, without an official ecclesiastical mandate. We already have associations of this kind in the Church; for example, the Knights of Columbus, the St. Vincent de Paul Society, the Serra Club, the pro-life movement, Marriage Encounter, the charismatic prayer groups, and the various scholarly and professional societies.

There are some necessary restrictions and qualifications, however, and the first is that the Christian faithful are encouraged to join associations that are already established and recommended by ecclesiastical authority. This is primarily to avoid the unnecessary proliferation of associations in the Church. Another prudent suggestion would be to foster national rather than diocesan organizations, as in the case of a Catholic television network or associations of and for the priests or the laity. Yet another restriction, repeated in canon 300, is that no association can identify itself as a "Catholic" organization without the consent of the proper ecclesiastical authority. Finally, we note that only the competent ecclesiastical authority can erect associations for the purpose of teaching Catholic doctrine in the name of the Church, for promoting public worship, or for engaging in any activity that is reserved to ecclesiastical authority. Of course, prudence would dictate that any group desiring to form a private association, free of any intervention from ecclesiastical authority, would make sure that they have the right to do so and at least inform the bishop or pastor of their intentions. In fact, canon 323 stipulates that the bishop should exercise vigilance over all autonomous associations.

> *CANON 217*: Since Christ's faithful are called by baptism to lead a life in harmony with the gospel teaching, they have the right to a Christian education which genuinely teaches them to strive for the maturity of the human person and at the same time to know and live the mystery of salvation.

It is in view of their obligation to live a good Christian life that all the faithful have the right to an education; and this, in turn, imposes a serious duty on parents and the pastors of the Church to provide the facilities for an education. Parents will educate their children primarily by the example of their own Christian lives and by the social interaction of the family. But both parents and their children rightly look to the ecclesiastical authorities to take the lead in promoting and providing Christian education. They are right to do so, since we read in canon 794:

> The Church has in a special way the duty and the right of educating, for it has a divine mission of helping all to arrive at the fullness of Christian life.

> Pastors of souls have the duty of making all possible arrange-
> ments so that all the faithful may avail themselves of a Catholic
> education.

And what kind of education are the parents and pastors sup-
posed to provide? A catechism class for an hour or two once a week
is hardly fulfilling the requirement. And in view of the atmosphere
in many public schools today, we need more than ever to provide
parochial or regional Catholic schools. A strong and vibrant
Catholic school system, headed by dedicated personnel, is the
foundation for a strong and vibrant Catholic population. It is also
the seed-bed for vocations to the priesthood and religious life. The
charter for Catholic education is beautifully summarized in canon
795, although teachers and parents are strongly urged to read the
relatively short document on Christian education, issued by the
Second Vatican Council in 1965.

> Education must pay regard to the formation of the whole person,
> so that all may attain their eternal destiny and at the same time
> promote the common good of society. Children and young
> persons are therefore to be cared for in such a way that their
> physical, moral and intellectual talents may develop in a
> harmonious manner, so that they may attain a greater sense of
> responsibility and a right use of freedom, and be formed to take
> an active part in social life.

The foregoing canon is taken from a lengthy section in the
Code of Canon Law that treats of Catholic education (canons 793 to
821) and it covers all the levels of education, from the elementary
school to the university. The canons that are pertinent to our
discussion are those that deal with the rights and duties of Catholic
parents. First of all, canon 793 states that parents have the right and
the duty to see to the education of their children, and Catholic
parents have the right and duty to provide a Catholic education.
Consequently, parents have the right to make use of any help

offered by the civil government in the area of education. Unfortunately, in countries where there is a severe separation between Church and State the government may provide education in public schools but refuse to contribute to any institution that is affiliated to some religion. In that case there is an added burden placed on the parents who are determined to give their children a Catholic education. It also poses a greater challenge to ecclesiastical authorities to see to it that Catholic schools are established. For that reason, canon 797 urges all the faithful to insist that the civil government find ways to protect and support the Catholic school system. Since the parents should be free in the selection of schools for their children, "Christ's faithful must be watchful that the civil society acknowledges this freedom of parents and, in accordance with the requirements of distributive justice, even provides them with assistance." They are also urged (canon 799) to make sure that the civil laws that regulate the education of the young should provide a religious and moral education that is in accord with the conscience of the parents. And in view of the fact that many men and women religious have abandoned the apostolate of teaching, it is interesting to note that canon 801 commands religious institutes that have education as their mission in the Church to preserve this mission faithfully and dedicate themselves to Catholic education.

> *CANON 218*: Those who are engaged in fields of sacred study have a just freedom to research matters in which they are expert and to express themselves prudently concerning them, with due allegiance to the magisterium of the Church.

In the past, this canon would have applied almost exclusively to seminarians and the clergy, since they were the ones who were engaged in the study of sacred doctrine on a professional level. Today, however, the various Catholic universities and pontifical faculties are open to all the faithful who have the competence to pursue the study of sacred doctrine on that level. All are free to do research and to express their opinions.

There are, however, two requirements for the proper use of academic freedom in the sacred sciences. First of all, the individual should have the expertise to speak on a given matter or to formulate a personal opinion. The sacred sciences are so highly specialized today that one must be wary of expressing opinions on matters that are outside his or her area of specialization. Moreover, as we saw in canon 212, when expressing one's opinion there should always be due regard for the integrity of faith and morals, reverence toward ecclesiastical authority, consideration for the common good, and respect for the dignity of individual persons.

The second requirement for the proper exercise of academic freedom is respect for the teaching authority of the Church. This gives rise to the question of dissent from that teaching authority, which is a rather common occurrence since the Second Vatican Council. There has always been dissent among theologians and various schools of theology, especially as regards "open questions" in theology; that is, matters on which there has been no official pronouncement by the magisterium of the Church. But for a theologian to dissent publicly from official Church teaching is quite another matter. In 1979, in a document on catechetics in our time, Pope John Paul II warned that theologians and exegetes have a duty to take care that the faithful do not take as a certainty that which is only a matter of opinion or discussion among the experts. He also proposed as reliable summaries of the faith of the Church the various creeds, and especially the "Creed of the People of God," composed by Pope Paul VI. Moreover, canon 750 states quite clearly what all the faithful are bound to believe and defend:

> Those things are to be believed by divine and Catholic faith
> which are contained in the word of God as it has been written or
> handed down by tradition, that is, in the single deposit of faith
> entrusted to the Church, and which are at the same time proposed

as divinely revealed either by the solemn magisterium of the
Church, or by its ordinary and universal magisterium, which is
manifested by the common adherence of Christ's faithful under
the guidance of the sacred magisterium. All are therefore bound
to shun any contrary doctrines.

It is well to recall at this point that the teaching authority or
magisterium of the Church is exercised by the Holy Father, by the
bishops in an Ecumenical Council, or by the bishops throughout the
world in union with the Holy Father when they definitively declare
that some doctrine of faith or morals is to be believed by all the
faithful (canon 749). However, no doctrine is to be understood as
infallibly defined unless this is clearly demonstrated.

Coming now to the end of our discussion of the rights that are
common to all the members of the Church, we recall what we said
at the outset, namely, that sometimes there are limitations or
restrictions on the exercise of rights. Thus, canon 223 states:

> In exercising their rights, Christ's faithful, both individually and
> in associations, must take into account the common good of the
> Church, as well as the rights of others and their own duties to
> others.

> Ecclesiastical authority is entitled to regulate, in view of the
> common good, the exercise of rights which are proper to Christ's
> faithful.

When ecclesiastical authority regulates or restricts the exercise of rights enjoyed by the faithful in view of what is best for the
parish or diocese, for example, we should always presume that
such an action is justifiable and necessary. Problems arise, however, when there is a question of conflict of rights or when certain
rights are being denied unjustly. What is to be done if the right of
the faithful to receive the sacraments or to hear the word of God is
not being respected? Or what recourse do the laity have if the

pastors do not make provision for the Catholic education of the children? Finally, to whom do cloistered nuns turn if a bishop insists that they assume an apostolate in the diocese?

According to canon 221 all the members of the Church may "lawfully vindicate and defend the rights they enjoy in the Church, before the competent ecclesiastical forum." Furthermore, "if any members of Christ's faithful are summoned to trial by competent authority, they have the right to be judged according to the provisions of the law, to be applied with equity." But canon 1419 states that in every diocese, except for cases that are reserved to another tribunal, the bishop has judicial power and he can exercise it personally or by delegation to others. In practice, therefore, it is the bishop of the diocese who normally resolves cases concerning conflicts or unjust denial of rights. If, however, the bishop himself is the accused party, the case goes to Rome. Indeed, we read in canon 1417: "Because of the primacy of the Roman Pontiff, any of the faithful may either refer their case to, or introduce it before, the Holy See, whether the case be contentious or penal. They may do so at any grade of trial or at any stage of the suit." The weakness of the system, as pointed out by some canonists, is that it is the legislative power rather than the judicial power that makes the final judgment. What is needed in the Church, they say, and especially at the diocesan level, is a separate and more autonomous judicial system that will more effectively protect and defend the rights of the faithful. But if the bishop lives up to his title as shepherd of the diocese, leading and serving the faithful, and does not defer too much of his responsibility to others, the present system is still as defensible as is the judicial role of parents in a family.

From what we have seen thus far, it is evident that the *Code of Canon Law* and the documents of the Second Vatican Council have taken a great step forward in defining and defending the rights of all the members of the Church. In this respect the Church is in tune with the times, because the question of human rights has become a burning issue throughout the world. The rights of Christ's faithful are not to be understood as favors or privileges granted by ecclesiastical authority; rather, they stem from the individual's incorporation into Christ through baptism. But they are not absolute rights; they can be conditioned and restricted when the good of the Church as a whole — universally or locally — requires it.

Moreover, wherever there are rights, there are corresponding duties, whether it be the obligation to respect the rights of others or to fulfill certain conditions for the lawful exercise of a right. Thus, if the faithful have a right to receive the sacraments and to hear the word of God, then it is the duty of the clergy to provide those services; and if men have the right to aspire to the permanent diaconate, they have an obligation to fulfill the requirements for that ministry. In order to complete our treatment of the role of Christ's faithful in the Church, we turn now to a discussion of the obligations that are common to all the People of God, whether clergy, laity or consecrated persons.

DUTIES OF THE CHRISTIAN FAITHFUL

We have deliberately treated of the rights of the faithful before coming to a discussion of their obligations. One could validly use either approach, since obligations give rise to rights and rights are the basis of subsequent duties, but the documents of the Second Vatican Council so frequently emphasize the basic equality of Christ's faithful and their sharing in his priestly, prophetic and kingly functions that it seemed more logical and more encouraging to treat first of the rights that flow from the sacrament of baptism.

> *CANON 209*:   Christ's faithful are bound to preserve their communion with the Church at all times, even in their external actions.

> They are to carry out with great diligence their responsibilities
> towards both the universal Church and the particular Church to
> which by law they belong.

This is a general statement concerning the obligation of all
baptized Christians to remain in union with the Church and to be
diligent in fulfilling their duties as members of the People of God.
What these duties are in particular can be found in various sections
of the *Code of Canon Law*, but we shall confine our discussion to
the more general treatment found in canons 209 to 223.

The first thing to be noted is that communion with the Church
is maintained, as we have already seen, by faith in the teaching of
the Church, worthy reception of the sacraments and obedience to
ecclesiastical authority. To be remiss in any one of these requirements is to weaken or destroy one's communion with the Church.
In fact, canon 212, 1, reminds the Christian faithful that they "are
bound to show Christian obedience to what the sacred Pastors, who
represent Christ, declare as teachers of the faith and prescribe as
rulers of the Church."

Secondly, all the members of the Church, regardless of their
class or state in life, have an obligation to be in union with the
Church "even in their external actions." In other words, it does not
suffice to be merely a Sunday Mass Catholic; one should give
witness to his or her Catholic faith on every day of the week and in
every situation. To fail to live up to one's religious belief is to
weaken the communion of the Church as a whole instead of
building up the Body of Christ. The scandal given by those who fail
to live up to their Christian vocation is one of the greatest obstacles
to successful evangelization. On the other hand, those Christians
who are faithful to the duties of their state of life — as priests, as
religious or as laity — are like spiritual magnets that attract and
draw others to the Church of Christ.

Finally, canon 209 speaks of the obligation of the faithful to
both the universal Church and the particular Church to which they

belong. One lives his or her Catholic life in the confines of the parish or the diocese and there is a strong tendency to define one's Catholic identity in terms of his or her nationality or culture. Increasingly we hear, for example, of the American Catholic Church, the African Catholic Church, the Filipino Catholic Church, etc. While there is a basis for speaking in this way, because of the process of enculturation by which the Christian life, and especially the liturgy, will be modified by the traditions, customs and institutions of a given people, there is always the danger of an excessively nationalistic attitude. This can lead to divisive tendencies or tensions among the various local churches or a separatist attitude toward the Holy See. The dictum of "unity without uniformity and pluralism without division" is applicable here. The Second Vatican Council touched on this matter in its document on the Church in the modern world, which is perhaps the document that best conveys the pastoral spirit of the Council.

> There are many links between the message of salvation and culture. In his self-revelation to his people, culminating in the fullness of manifestation in his incarnate Son, God spoke according to the culture proper to each age. Similarly the Church has existed through the centuries in varying circumstances and has utilized the resources of different cultures in its preaching to spread and explain the message of Christ, to examine and understand it more deeply, and to express it more perfectly in the liturgy and in various aspects of the life of the faithful.

> Nevertheless, the Church has been sent to all ages and nations and, therefore, is not tied exclusively and indissolubly to any race or nation, to any one particular way of life, or to any customary practices, ancient or modern. The Church is faithful to its traditions and is at the same time conscious of its universal mission; it can, then, enter into communion with different forms of culture, thereby enriching both itself and the cultures themselves.

The good news of Christ continually renews the life and culture of fallen man; it combats and removes the error and evil which flow from the ever-present attraction of sin. It never ceases to purify and elevate the morality of peoples. It takes the spiritual qualities and endowments of every age and nation and, with supernatural riches, it causes them to blossom, as it were, from within; it fortifies, completes and restores them in Christ. In this way the Church carries out its mission and in that very act it stimulates and advances human and civil culture, as well as contributing by its activity, including liturgical activity, to man's interior freedom.

For the reasons given above, the Church recalls to mind that culture must be subordinated to the integral development of the human person, to the good of the community and of the whole of mankind. (GS 58)

In the *Dogmatic Constitution on the Church* the Second Vatican Council states several times that the vocation of Christ's faithful is not only a call to share in the apostolic mission of the Church but it is also a vocation to holiness. "All the faithful," says the document, "whatever their condition or state — though each in his own way — are called by the Lord to that perfection of sanctity by which the Father himself is perfect." And later we read: "All Christians in any state or walk of life are called to the fullness of Christian life and to the perfection of love, and by this holiness a more human manner of life is fostered also in earthly society." This same teaching is repeated in the *Code of Canon Law*, but with an added reference to the obligation of all Christ's faithful to participate in the mission of the Church.

CANON 210:   All Christ's faithful, each according to his or her own condition, must make a wholehearted effort to lead a holy life, and to promote the growth of the Church and its continual sanctification.

CANON 211:   All Christ's faithful have the obligation and the right to strive so that the divine message of salvation may more and more reach all people of all times and all places.

There is, therefore, a double dimension to the vocation of the Christian faithful. Each and every member of the People of God is called to strive for the perfection of charity and also to participate actively in the mission of the Church, according to his or her condition and state of life. No doubt many Catholics, and especially among the laity, were startled to hear that they are called to holiness of life and, indeed, that they have an obligation to work toward the perfection of their personal lives. For centuries they had been led to believe — thanks to the teaching of some theologians — that the words of Christ, "You therefore are to be perfect even as your heavenly Father is perfect," were addressed only to the clergy and religious. The ordinary Christian could attain nothing more than a so-called "ascetical" perfection in the Christian life; that is, to live in the state of grace in obedience to the commandments and to cultivate the virtues proper to one's state in life. Anything beyond that would be out of the ordinary and not to be sought after. The result of such teaching was to set up two distinct types of perfection, one for the ordinary Christian and the other for the exceptional and rare individual. But thanks to the teaching of theologians such as John G. Arintero, O.P., Reginald Garrigou-Lagrange, O.P., Gabriel of St. Mary Magdalen, O.C.D., and Jacques Maritain, the traditional spiritual doctrine was restored and eventually promulgated by the Second Vatican Council:

The Lord Jesus, divine teacher and model of all perfection, preached holiness of life (of which he is the author and maker) to each and every one of his disciples without distinction: "You therefore must be perfect, as your heavenly Father is perfect" (Mt 5:48). For he sent the Holy Spirit to all to move them

interiorly to love God with their whole heart, with their whole
soul, with their whole understanding, and with their whole
strength (cf. Mk 12:30), and to love one another as Christ loved
them (cf. Jn 13:34; 15:12). (LG 40)

Even in the earliest days of the Church St. Paul did not hesitate
to tell the Thessalonians: "It is God's will that you grow in
holiness" (1 Th 4:3). If we have been incorporated into Christ
through baptism, then we receive the life of grace through him and
can share in the holiness that is his. Moreover, if one of the marks
of the Church of Christ is holiness, then as members of that
Mystical Body we also should be holy. All Christians, therefore,
fall under the precept to strive for the perfection of charity, but not
all in the same measure. The clergy, those consecrated to God by
the evangelical counsels, and parents of families are among those
who have a special obligation to give witness to holiness of life, but
all the People of God should strive to become the holy People of
God. "The forms and tasks of life are many, but holiness is
one. . . . Each one, however, according to his own gifts and duties
must steadfastly advance along the way of a living faith, which
arouses hope and works through love." This statement in the
Second Vatican Council's document on the Church corrects two
erroneous opinions concerning Christian perfection and holiness.
First, the pursuit of Christian perfection is not the exclusive obligation of clergy and religious; it is the duty of all Christians. Secondly, the attainment of Christian perfection and holiness is not an
extraordinary gift granted to a few chosen souls, while all others
must be content with the lower "ordinary" way; rather, the one
and the same holiness — the perfection of love of God and
neighbor — is offered to all, so that Christian perfection is within
the "normal" development of the life of grace and charity. Holiness and perfection are not determined primarily by one's state of
life but by the intensity of one's love of God and neighbor.

Closely related to the vocation to holiness is the duty to

participate actively in the mission of the Church. From this obligation to be involved in some form of evangelization flow many of the rights that we have already discussed; for example, the right to form associations, the right to a Catholic education, the right to be engaged in apostolic activity, etc. In recent years great emphasis has been placed on the fact that the Church is a missionary Church. At the close of the Holy Year in 1975 Pope Paul VI stated: ''The command that was given to the Twelve: 'Go preach the Gospel' applies to all Christians, though in different ways.''

We cannot defer the work of evangelization and apostolate to the clergy and religious any more than we can place on them alone the obligation to strive for Christian perfection. Everyone in the Church must in one way or another be an apostle; this is both a duty and a right.

The most common form of evangelization, available to every good Christian, is the example of one's own life and Christian witness. People are often more influenced, in an intuitive and non-verbal way, by what we are and do than by anything we may say. Other forms of evangelization will be determined by one's condition, state of life or office in the Church. But regardless of what the specific ministry or apostolate may be, it should flow from one's personal holiness, which is measured by the degree of one's love of God and of neighbor in God. If there is no place among the People of God for a purely individualistic, passive Christianity, neither is there room for the heresy of activism.

> *CANON 222*:   Christ's faithful have the obligation to provide for the needs of the Church, so that the Church has available to it those things which are necessary for divine worship, for apostolic and charitable work and for the worthy support of its ministers.
>
> They are also obliged to promote social justice and, mindful of the Lord's precept, to help the poor from their own resources.

This final canon on the obligations common to all the members of Christ's faithful deals with the support necessary for the various activities of the Church. Although one would logically think first of financial support, the fact is that there are many other ways of contributing to the needs of the Church. One may, for example, provide voluntary service in the parish or diocese or in some Catholic institution; or it may be a question of donating goods, as when a bakery sends the weekly supply of bread to an orphanage or a monastery of cloistered nuns.

The needs of a parish or diocese normally fall into three categories: divine worship and liturgy, apostolic and charitable works, and a decent livelihood for the clergy. We are not forgetting, of course, the needs of the Vatican and the Roman Curia, which are supplied in part by the Peter's Pence collection throughout the world, or the occasional contributions requested by the National Conference of Bishops. However, for the average Catholic it is the local parish or diocese that is usually the recipient of his or her contribution in terms of money, goods, time or talent.

Obviously, the obligation to support the Church falls largely on the laity, although we should not overlook the contributions made by the clergy and various religious institutes in terms of time, talent and personnel. In fact, canon 282, after advising the clergy to lead a simple life, encourages them to use for the good of the Church and charitable works anything that is ''over and above what is necessary for their worthy upkeep and the fulfillment of all the duties of their state.'' Religious, on the other hand, do not have free administration of money and temporal goods, but their particular Order or Congregation may well be in a position to donate to the missions or works of charity.

There is, in addition, a good reason why the support of the Church falls principally on the laity. The Church has to own and administer certain goods and property in order to carry on its mission, but, as we have seen, the Church's mission does not rest exclusively on the shoulders of the bishops and priests; the laity also have an obligation to take an active part. Moreover, it is the laity who are directly involved in temporal affairs and have greater access to the goods and wealth of the world.

Unfortunately, both in the Church and in the world people are under an ever greater economic strain. As a result, statistics show that there has been a notable decrease in donations to the Church and to charitable works. More and more the various projects under Church auspices are dependent on the generosity of wealthy individuals or the foundations set up by large corporations. On the other hand, given the constantly rising inflation and the exorbitant cost of education, medical care, and the maintenance of religious institutions, the only alternative in many cases is to close parishes or sell Catholic institutions that can no longer support themselves. Yet one would hope that before such drastic steps are taken, someone would ask whether it has to cost so much to carry on the mission of the Church or whether we can find generous and apostolic Christians who are willing to give their time and talent in return for a more modest salary.

Our final comment on canon 222 concerns the twofold obligation of all Christ's faithful to work for social justice and help the poor out of their own resources. As regards the promotion of social justice, various popes in this century have called upon the faithful to become aware of the problems of social, economic and racial injustice. The present Holy Father, Pope John Paul II has continued in this same tradition by emphasizing the dignity of the human person and calling for solidarity. Catholics can point with pride to the bishops, priests, religious and laity who have marched shoulder to shoulder with those who are fighting for racial equality and for the right to life of the unborn.

In addition to promoting social justice, the faithful of Christ are obliged to assist the poor "out of their own resources." Canon 222 mentions "the precept of the Lord" in this connection, and perhaps the anecdote about the rich young man comes to mind. He had asked the Lord what he should do in addition to observing the Commandments, and the Lord said: "If you seek perfection, go, sell your possessions, and give to the poor." That, however, was not given by Jesus as a precept but as an invitation to practice evangelical poverty, and the young man did not accept it. The precept of the Lord that applies to our obligation to help the poor is found in chapter 5 of the Gospel according to Matthew. "For I was hungry and you gave me food, I was thirsty and you gave me drink, I was a stranger and you welcomed me, naked and you clothed me. . . . Lord, when did we see you hungry and feed you or see you thirsty and give you drink? When did we welcome you away from home or clothe you in your nakedness? . . . I assure you, as often as you did it for one of my least brothers, you did it for me." We have here the leitmotif of the spirituality and apostolate of that great angel of charity, Mother Teresa of Calcutta.

This canon implicitly reminds Christ's faithful that while it is praiseworthy to donate funds to the various Church agencies for the relief of the poor, Christ also wants us to help one another on the personal level of fraternal charity. He told us that the poor will always be with us; therefore there are countless occasions in daily life when the empty hand of the needy is extended to us. We have the example of St. Martin of Tours and St. Vincent de Paul to remind us that in serving the poor, we are serving Christ.

* * * * * * * *

We have now completed our survey of the nature and mission of the Church and the role of the faithful of Christ as the People of God. In looking more closely at the various classes of Christ's faithful — clergy, consecrated persons and laity — we have necessarily treated at some length of the rights and duties that are common to everyone without distinction. The fact that we are now able to have such an all-embracing concept of the Church is due in no small measure to the work of the Fathers of the Second Vatican

Council. We can no longer think of the Church as the hierarchy or the Vatican; rather, all together — clergy, consecrated persons and laity — can say: ''We are the Church.''

CHAPTER 3

THE LAITY

Up to this point we have looked at the Church as the People of God, and the members of the Church as the faithful of Christ, in whom they are incorporated through baptism to share in his priestly, prophetic and kingly functions. The emphasis has been on the basic equality of all baptized Christians and the rights and duties that are common to all without distinction. These same ideas are beautifully summarized by the Second Vatican Council in its document on the Church:

> There is, therefore, one chosen People of God: ''one Lord, one faith, one baptism'' (Ep 4:5); there is a common dignity of members deriving from their rebirth in Christ, a common grace as sons, a common vocation to perfection, one salvation, one hope and undivided charity. In Christ and in the Church there is, then, no inequality arising from race or nationality, social condition or sex, for ''there is neither Jew nor Greek; there is neither slave nor freeman; there is neither male nor female. For you are all one in Christ Jesus'' (Gal 3:28; cf. Col 3 :11).
>
> In the Church not everyone marches along the same path, yet all are called to sanctity and have obtained an equal privilege of faith through the justice of God (cf. 2 P 1:1). Although by Christ's will some are established as teachers, dispensers of the mysteries and pastors for the others, there remains, nevertheless,

> a true equality among all with regard to the dignity and to the
> activity which is common to all the faithful in the building up of
> the Body of Christ. . . . And so amid variety all will bear witness
> to the wonderful unity in the Body of Christ: this very diversity
> of graces, of ministries and of works gathers the sons of God into
> one, for "all these things are the work of the one and the same
> Spirit" (1 Cor 12:11). (LG 32)

This statement is of crucial importance for understanding the
nature and role of the laity in the Church and in the world. In the
first place, it helps us see the distinction between the Church as the
People of God and the Church as the Mystical Body of Christ.
Moreover, it establishes the basis for distinguishing between the
vocation and the mission of the laity, the clergy and those in the
consecrated life. All baptized Christians have the same vocation;
they are called to strive for the perfection of charity. Similarly, all
baptized Christians are commanded to participate actively in the
life and mission of the Church. Therefore any diversity or distinction among the various classes of Christ's faithful must come, not
from their incorporation in Christ through baptism or their vocation
to holiness, but from the particular function, office or mission that
they have in the Church. Such was the teaching of St. Paul:

> Just as each of us has one body with many members, and not all
> the members have the same function, so too we, though many,
> are one body in Christ and individually members of one another.
> (Rm 12:4-5; cf. 1 Cor 12-31)

In the same context St. Augustine told the Christians of his
day: "When I am frightened by what I am to you, then I am
consoled by what I am with you. To you I am the bishop, with you I
am a Christian. The first is an office, the second a grace; the first a
danger, the second salvation." That was his way of saying that in

the Church there is one vocation and one mission common to all of Christ's faithful, but that each one will pursue these goals according to his or her condition and state of life.

TOWARDS A DEFINITION OF THE LAITY

We have already seen that canon 207 of the *Code of Canon Law* states that by divine institution there are two classes of the faithful of Christ: the clergy and the laity, and that those in the consecrated life are drawn from these two classes. It is easy enough to define the clergy: they are those baptized Christians who have received the sacrament of holy orders and are deputed for the sacred ministry as deacons, priests or bishops in the Church. Those in the consecrated life, on the other hand, are those Christians who have separated themselves from temporal pursuits by making a vow or promise to live according to the evangelical counsels of poverty, chastity and obedience in an institute approved by ecclesiastical authority. But who are the laity?

Ordinarily we designate as a "lay person" anyone who is not a professional or expert in a given field or area of competence. Thus, a person who is not a medical doctor, research scientist, nuclear physicist or legal expert would be classified as a lay person in relation to those professions. In like manner, a Catholic who is not a deacon, priest or bishop is a lay Christian. To define the Catholic laity as those who are not members of the clergy is a negative definition, but it does not in any way imply a downgrading or disdain for the laity. It is simply a statement of the fact that laity are not clergy, and one could just as rightly define clergy as those who are not laity. In like manner, to describe the diocesan priest as a priest who is not a religious does not necessarily imply that he is therefore a priest of lesser rank or dignity. Unfortunately, negative definitions are often interpreted as being based on bias or prejudice, as would be the case if one were to define a woman as a human being who is not a man. All the more reason, then, for attempting to formulate a definition of the laity that will be positive and theological.

An accurate definition should first of all state the genus or class to which the defined object belongs; then it should identify the specific difference that sets that object apart from every other member of the genus. For example, a human being is correctly defined as a rational animal, since human beings are in the class or genus of animal but are differentiated from all other animals by their rationality; i.e., they are endowed with the spiritual faculties of intellect and will.

We have already seen that in the early Church the Greek word for laity designated the People of God indiscriminately and until modern times the word "laity" was used interchangeably with "the faithful." That is no longer correct usage, however, since the documents of the Second Vatican Council use the term "the faithful of Christ" to apply to all the members of the Church: clergy, laity and consecrated persons. Moreover, when the *Code of Canon Law* refers to the laity specifically, it frequently uses the expression "the lay faithful" or "lay members of Christ's faithful." This means that while the laity are as much members of Christ's faithful as are the clergy and consecrated persons, since they are all incorporated into Christ through baptism, there is a specific, particular characteristic that is proper to the laity precisely because they are lay members of Christ's faithful. What is this specific difference that sets the laity apart, so to speak, from the clergy and consecrated persons? It has been clearly stated in the *Dogmatic Constitution on the Church*:

> Their secular character is proper and peculiar to the laity. . . .
> By reason of their special vocation it belongs to the laity to seek
> the kingdom of God by engaging in temporal affairs and direct-
> ing them according to God's will. They live in the world, that is,
> they are engaged in each and every work and business of the

earth and in the ordinary circumstances of social and family life which, as it were, constitute their very existence. There they are called by God that, being led by the Spirit to the Gospel, they may contribute to the sanctification of the world, as from within like leaven, by fulfilling their own particular duties. . . . The laity, however, are given this special vocation: to make the Church present and fruitful in those places and circumstances where it is only through them that she can become the salt of the earth. (LG 31)

Consequently, we can describe the laity as those members of Christ's faithful whose specific role in the mission of the Church is to sanctify the temporal order, the world in which they live. The particular mission of the laity in the Church — to sanctify the temporal order — is the specific difference that distinguishes the laity from the clergy and persons in the consecrated life. However, one must be careful not to place in opposition the secular character of the laity and their active participation in the Church. As early as 1930 Msgr. Escrivá, the founder of Opus Dei, stated: "To concentrate solely on the specific secular mission of the layman and forget his membership in the Church would be as absurd as to imagine a green branch in full bloom which did not belong to any tree. But to forget what is specific and proper to the layman, or to misunderstand the characteristics of his apostolic tasks and their value to the Church, would be to reduce the flourishing tree of the Church to the monstrous condition of a barren trunk" (*Conversations*, p. 22).

In view of the foregoing balanced statement, we cannot agree with those canonists who maintain that it suffices to describe the laity in terms of the rights and duties that they have in common with all the other Christian faithful; that we should not try to identify the laity as a distinct class. But that would blur the image of the laity in the Church and once again reduce them to an amorphous mass with no specific identity. It would be like defining a human being as simply an animal and neglecting to add that the human being is an animal endowed with the spiritual faculties of intellect and will. Fortunately, Pope John Paul II has developed the teaching of the Second Vatican Council in his post-Synodal exhortation, issued in December, 1988. His remarks on the secular character of the laity deserve careful attention:

> Because of the one dignity flowing from baptism, each member of the lay faithful, together with ordained ministers and men and women religious, shares a responsibility for the Church's mission.
>
> But among the lay faithful this one baptismal dignity takes on *a manner of life which sets a person apart, without, however, bringing about a separation* from the ministerial priesthood or from men and women religious. The Second Vatican Council has described this manner of life as the ''secular character'': ''The secular character is properly and particularly that of the lay faithful.''
>
> To understand properly the lay faithful's position in the Church in a complete, adequate and specific manner it is necessary to come to a deeper theological understanding of their secular character in light of God's plan of salvation and in the context of the mystery of the Church.
>
> Pope Paul VI said the Church ''has an authentic secular dimension, inherent to her inner nature and mission, which is deeply rooted in the mystery of the Word Incarnate, and which is realized in different forms through her members.''
>
> The Church, in fact, lives in the world, even if she is not of the world (cf. Jn 17:16). She is sent to continue the redemptive work of Jesus Christ, which ''by its very nature concerns the salvation of humanity, and also involves the renewal of the whole temporal order.''

Certainly *all the members of the Church* are sharers in this
secular dimension but *in different ways*. In particular the sharing
of the *lay faithful* has its own manner of realization and function,
which, according to the Council, is "properly and particularly"
theirs. Such a manner is designated with the expression "secular
character."

*The "world" thus becomes the place and the means for the lay
faithful to fulfill their Christian vocation,* because the world
itself is destined to glorify the Father in Christ. . . . Thus, for the
lay faithful, to be present and active in the world is not only an
anthropological and sociological reality, but in a specific way, a
theological and ecclesiological reality as well.

The lay faithful's *position in the Church*, then, comes to be
fundamentally defined by their *newness in Christian life* and
distinguished by their *secular character*. (CL 15)

To summarize: the laity, like all other members of Christ's
faithful, are baptized persons (sacramental aspect) who are thereby
incorporated into Christ (Christian aspect) and made members of
the Church (ecclesiological aspect) with the right and duty to
participate actively in the mission of the Church (missionary aspect). But in addition to all that, the laity, by reason of their secular
characteristic, are committed to the renewal and sanctification of
the temporal order. The laity, therefore, have a mission in both the
temporal and the spiritual orders, but "they are nevertheless so
closely linked that God's plan is, in Christ, to take the whole world
up again and make of it a new creation" (AA 5).

There may, of course, be a temptation to establish an unwarranted dichotomy between the Church and the world, the sacred
and the profane, or the spiritual and the temporal. This has in fact
been done by some theologians and spiritual writers. But in the
lengthy quotation from the Apostolic Exhortation of Pope John
Paul II we have seen that secularity is the proper characteristic of

the laity precisely because the temporal order is intimately related
to the mission of the Church. That is why the Holy Father insisted
that the world is a theological and ecclesiological reality. Yves
Congar, O.P., a pioneer in developing a theology of the laity,
stated in 1950: ''Lay people are called to the same end as clergy or
monks — to the enjoyment of our inheritance as sons of God; but
they have to pursue and attain this end without cutting down their
involvement in the activities of the world. . . . The laity are called
to do God's work in the world.''

Two other points are worthy of mention and deserving of
further study and development. The first point was touched upon
by Edward Schillebeeckx, O.P., in an article on the laity,
published in 1965: ''It has not yet been understood with sufficient
depth that, precisely because he is a non-clerical member of the
People of God, the layman has a constitutive relationship with the
secular world, which permeates also his participation in the
Church's primary mission. The result is that the layman's specific
contribution to the work of spreading the Gospel is undervalued
and, when he is genuinely active, he adopts clerical ways which
prejudice his character as an authentic layman.'' This same idea
was expressed by Pope John Paul II in 1984 when he spoke of the
tendency to clericalize the laity and laicize the clergy.

The second point has to do with the fact that various documents on the priesthood and the religious life have underlined the
sacred ministry as the primary function of the clergy and separation
from the world as a characteristic proper to religious. Since the
Second Vatican Council, however, more and more so-called
''hyphenated'' priests have become immersed in secular activities
and a large number of active religious have abandoned their traditional community lifestyle and observances. But perhaps with time
and experimentation something quite new will emerge in the
Church, as has happened in centuries past when new wine could
not be put in old wineskins.

DUTIES OF THE CHRISTIAN LAITY

CANON 224:   Lay members of Christ's faithful have the duties and rights enumerated in the canons of this title, in addition to those duties and rights which are common to all Christ's faithful and those stated in other canons.

Since the rights and duties common to all Christ's faithful are also applicable to the laity, there will necessarily be some repetition when we discuss the rights and duties that are listed in Canon Law under the title "The Obligations and Rights of the Lay Members of Christ's Faithful" (canons 224-231). Moreover, there are other canons throughout the *Code* that pertain to the laity, and we shall refer to them as the need arises. As we did in speaking of the rights and duties common to all the members of the Church, we shall again follow rather closely the *Code of Canon Law*, although not necessarily in the order that the various canons are listed. We do this because it is in the *Code* that we find the most recent (1983) body of laws by which the universal Church is governed. Also, as we have already noted, the canonical legislation of the Church is an authentic echo of the teaching of the Vatican II Ecumenical Council.

In this first canon we have an explicit distinction between the expression "Christ's faithful" and the term "lay members of Christ's faithful." The clergy and persons in the consecrated life are also Christ's faithful and therefore the term applies to all the People of God without exception. But it may take some time for people — and especially the clergy — to stop applying the term "the faithful" exclusively to the laity.

CANON 225:   Since lay people, like all Christ's faithful, are deputed to the apostolate by baptism and confirmation, they are bound by the general obligation and they have the right, whether

> as individuals or in associations, to strive so that the divine message of salvation may be known and accepted by all people throughout the world. This obligation is all the more insistent in circumstances in which only through them are people able to hear the Gospel and to know Christ.

> They have also, according to the condition of each, the special obligation to permeate and perfect the temporal order of things with the spirit of the Gospel. In this way, particularly in conducting secular business and exercising secular functions, they are to give witness to Christ.

By reason of their baptism and confirmation all the faithful of Christ have an obligation to participate actively in the mission of the Church, each one according to his or her condition or state of life. The mission of the Church, as we have seen, is the one given it by Christ: to bring the Gospel message to all nations. Consequently, the laity have a definite role to play in the evangelization that is carried out in the name of Christ and his Church. Canon 225 states succinctly and clearly the areas of apostolic activity that are peculiarly proper to the lay members of the faithful of Christ. Indeed, the content of this canon is the basis for all further development and application of a theology of the mission of the laity in the Church and in the world.

The lay Christian is, as it were, a citizen of two worlds: the Church and civil society, and in both of them he has specific rights and duties. The Second Vatican Council took note of this twofold aspect of the laity's vocation and mission in its document on the Church: "The laity should learn to distinguish carefully between the rights and the duties which they have as belonging to the Church and those which fall to them as members of the human society. They will strive to unite the two harmoniously, remembering that in every temporal affair they are to be guided by a Christian conscience, since not even in temporal business may any human activity be withdrawn from God's dominion" (LG 36).

The active participation of the laity in the Church's mission to bring the Gospel message to all nations is a vocation and a duty that come from Christ himself. For that reason the Fathers of the Second Vatican Council reminded the bishops to be sure that the laity are involved in Church affairs and to recognize the right and duty of the laity ''to play their part in building up the Mystical Body of Christ.''

Like all the other members of the Church, the laity have the right to exercise their particular apostolate either individually or in associations of some kind. But they are not obliged to join any particular association or society. In fact, in its document on the laity the Second Vatican Council takes special care to emphasize the importance of the individual lay apostolate:

> The apostolate to be exercised by the individual . . . is the starting point and condition of all types of lay apostolate, including the organized apostolate; nothing can replace it.

> The individual apostolate is everywhere and always in place; in certain circumstances it is the only one appropriate, the only one possible. Every lay person, whatever his condition, is called to it, is obliged to it, even if he has not the opportunity or possibility of collaborating in associations. (AA 16)

The principal means by which the Church brings the message of Christ to the world is by the ministry of the word (preaching and teaching) and by the ministry of the sacraments, which are channels of grace and life. These two ministries are committed in a special way to the clergy, because only those in holy orders are authorized to perform the sacred ministries. But we read in the foregoing document on the laity that ''laymen have countless opportunities for exercising the apostolate of evangelization and sanctification. The very witness of a Christian life, and good works done in a supernatural spirit, are effective in drawing men to the faith and to God'' (AA 6).

When canon 225 states that the obligation to engage in the lay apostolate is "all the more insistent in circumstances in which only through the laity are people able to hear the Gospel and to know Christ," it is simply repeating what the Council's document on the Church had already said: "The laity, however, are given this special vocation: to make the Church present and fruitful in those places and circumstances where it is only through them that she can become the salt of the earth" (LG 33). This can be taken to mean that the laity have a special duty not only to bring Gospel values to the domestic, social, economic and political structures of the temporal order, but in case of necessity — and when authorized to do so — to collaborate with the hierarchy by performing functions that are normally reserved to the clergy.

However, the proper and preferential area for lay apostolate is the temporal order, and this has been insisted upon time and time again in various documents of the Second Vatican Council. But this apostolate requires that the laity be properly trained for their work in the world, whether in the various professions or in other structures and activities of the temporal order. In addition, and even more importantly as regards the apostolate, the laity will need a properly formed conscience, and this in turn requires at least a basic education in Christian truths and moral values. Consequently, in the document on the laity the Fathers of the Second Vatican Council made some very important observations:

> The hierarchy's duty is to favor the lay apostolate, furnish it with principles and spiritual assistance, direct the exercise of the apostolate to the common good of the Church, and see to it that doctrine and order are safeguarded. . . . As for works and institutions of the temporal order, the duty of the ecclesiastical hierarchy is the teaching and authentic interpretation of the moral principles to be followed in this domain. It is also in its province to judge, after mature reflection and with the help of qualified persons, of the conformity of such works or institutions

with moral principles, and to pronounce in their regard concerning what is required for the safeguard and promotion of the values of the supernatural order. (AA 24)

The role of ecclesiastical authority is confined to providing spiritual and moral guidance to the laity in the area of their secular competence, but the clergy have an obligation to respect the right of the lay Christians to exercise personal responsibility and freedom in dealing with temporal matters. On the other hand, the laity must not put forth as Catholic teaching what is merely a matter of opinion nor should they invoke the authority of the Church to promote their own particular point of view.

In his Apostolic Exhortation on evangelization in the modern world (1975), Pope Paul VI made special reference to the role of the laity in the mission of the Church:

> Laymen, whose vocation commits them to the world and to various temporal enterprises, should exercise a special form of evangelization.
>
> Their principal and primary function is not to establish or promote ecclesial communities, which is the special function of pastors, but to develop and make effective all those latent Christian and evangelical possibilities which already exist and operate in the world.
>
> The special field for their evangelical zeal is the wide and complex arena of politics, sociology and economics. They can be effective also in the spheres of culture, the sciences, the arts, international relations and the communications media. There are certain other fields which are especially appropriate for evangelization such as human love, the family, the education of children and adolescents, the practice of the various professions and the relief of human suffering. If laymen who are actively involved in these spheres are inspired with the evangelical spirit, if they are competent and are determined to bring into play all

those Christian powers in themselves which so often lie hidden
and dormant, then all these activities will be all the more helpful
in the building up of the kingdom of God and in bringing
salvation in Jesus Christ. And in this their effectiveness in the
temporal sphere will be in no way diminished; on the contrary,
new fields of higher achievement will be opened up to them.
(EN 70)

Thus, no area of human or even secular activity can be left
untouched by the Christian influence. Pope John Paul II has stated
that the entire mission of the Church is concentrated in evangelization, and in speaking of the laity in his Apostolic Exhortation on the
1987 Synod, he says that "their responsibility, in particular, is to
testify how the Christian faith constitutes the only fully valid
response . . . to the problems and hopes that life poses to every
person and society. This will be possible if the lay faithful will
know how to overcome in themselves the separation of the Gospel
from life, to again take up in their daily activities in family, work
and society, an integrated approach to life that is fully brought
about by the inspiration and strength of the Gospel'' (CL 34).

CANON 226:   Those who are married are bound by the special
obligation, in accordance with their own vocation, to strive for
the building up of the people of God through their marriage and
family.

Because they gave life to their children, parents have the most
serious obligation and the right to educate them. It is therefore
primarily the responsibility of Christian parents to ensure the
Christian education of their children in accordance with the
teaching of the Church.

Marriage is both a special vocation and a sacrament. Indeed,
it is the normal state of life for men and women, because God
created man and woman for each other and for the procreation of

the human race. There is thus a twofold aspect to marriage. It is first of all a covenant of generous love between a man and a woman who vow to share their entire lives with one another. Secondly, as we read in the Vatican II document on the Church in the modern world, marriage and marital love are "ordered to the procreation and education of the offspring and it is in them that it finds its crowning glory" (GS 48).

Since marriage is the normal vocation for men and women, every person has a right to marry if he or she is suited for married life, although one may choose to remain in the single state. Moreover, since marriage constitutes a permanent and stable state of life, the duties incumbent on spouses and parents take precedence over every other pursuit or activity. This means that the first obligation of married persons is to their own home and family, which the Second Vatican Council has called "the domestic church." A person who neglects his or her family, even for religious or apostolic activity, is thereby failing to live up to the duties of state in life. Pope John Paul II has stated in his post-Synodal document of 1988 that even the duty of the laity to society at large begins primarily in the family, and hence the need for married people to be convinced of the "unique and irreplaceable value that the family has in the development of society and the Church itself" (CL 40).

The second paragraph of canon 226 is addressed to parents, reminding them of their serious obligation and their right to educate their children. It is therefore primarily the obligation of parents to see to it that their children receive a Christian education. There are numerous other canons that touch on this same subject — an indication of how serious is the obligation to provide a Christian education for one's children. For example, canons 776 and 777 remind parish priests of their duty to provide religious instruction, and canon 778 says the same thing to religious superiors and others who staff parishes or schools. Canons 793 and 814 deal precisely with Catholic schools and contain important legislation that pertains to parents, parish priests, religious and bishops.

In referring to the right and duty of parents to educate their children and to make sure that they are formed in accordance with the teaching of the Church, canon 226 is not restricting itself to academic education. If the parents are the primary educators of their children, this education should start some years before the children begin to attend school. In some ways those early years are the most crucial in relation to the child's development and growth into a mature adult. Consequently, parents — and also older children in the family — should first and continually help to educate the children through the example of a good Christian life. Then, as the children grow, the parents are urged to take an active part in preparing them for the reception of the various sacraments — penance, Eucharist, confirmation, marriage. The long-lasting effects of one's early education and training have been described by Dorothy Law Nolte under the title, "A Child Learns What He Lives":

If a child lives with criticism, he learns to condemn.

If a child lives with hostility, he learns to fight.

If a child lives with ridicule, he learns to be shy.

If a child lives with shame, he learns to feel guilty.

If a child lives with tolerance, he learns to be patient.

If a child lives with encouragement, he learns confidence.

If a child lives with praise, he learns to appreciate.

If a child lives with fairness, he learns justice.

If a child lives with security, he learns to have faith.

If a child lives with approval, he learns to like himself.

If a child lives with acceptance and friendship, he learns to find love in the world.

The last canon in this section that treats of the duties of the laity in particular is the first paragraph of canon 231, and it reads as follows:

CANON 231, #1: Lay people who are pledged to the special service of the Church, whether permanently or for a time, have a duty to acquire the appropriate formation which their role demands, so that they may conscientiously, earnestly and diligently fulfill this role.

It goes without saying that in general any person who performs an activity or service should have the competence to do so, whether it be related to the Church or a secular profession. The lay members of the Church are now capable of performing a variety of services that were formerly reserved to the clergy. Most noteworthy has been the admission of the laity to active participation in liturgical ministries and in certain areas of ecclesiastical government. This canon, therefore, does not apply to the lay apostolate in the strict sense of the word (although there, too, one would expect that individuals have the competence to perform their tasks); we have already seen that the laity have freedom and autonomy in their own secular and domestic domain. Canon 231 refers to those lay persons who are ''pledged to some special service to the Church,'' and consequently come under the jurisdiction of ecclesiastical authority. The regulations of this canon would apply, for example, to catechists and teachers of religion, pastoral associates, auxiliary chaplains and counselors in Church institutions, directors of Catholic lay organizations, lectors and acolytes and leaders of Church music, extraordinary ministers of the Eucharist, and those who hold positions in the government and administration of a parish or diocese. On the other hand, the canon implies that there is a concomitant obligation for priests and bishops to make provision for the proper formation and education of lay persons deputed to any of the above-mentioned functions or offices in the Church.

RIGHTS OF THE CHRISTIAN LAITY

In its document on the missionary activity of the Church the Second Vatican Council has strongly emphasized the need to foster a mature Christian laity: "The Church is not truly established and does not fully live nor is a perfect sign of Christ unless there is a genuine laity existing and working alongside the hierarchy. For the Gospel cannot become deeply rooted in the mentality, life and work of a people without the active presence of lay people" (GS 21).

The right and duty of the laity to participate actively in the mission of the Church is not a privilege or mandate given them by the hierarchy; rather, as we have seen, it stems from their incorporation into Christ through baptism, by which they also share in Christ's and the Church's priestly, prophetic and kingly functions. And although under particular circumstances the laity may be allowed to perform certain liturgical functions, the area of apostolic work that is most properly theirs is the temporal order. This is clearly stated in the revised *Code of Canon Law* and the documents of the Second Vatican Council.

> *CANON 227:*   To lay members of Christ's faithful belongs the
> right to have acknowledged as theirs that freedom in secular
> affairs which is common to all citizens. In using this freedom,
> however, they are to ensure that their actions are permeated with
> the spirit of the Gospel, and they are to heed the teaching of the
> Church proposed by the *magisterium*, but they must be on guard,
> in questions of opinion, against proposing their own view as the
> teaching of the Church.

To those of the faithful who enjoy full religious freedom, it may seem unnecessary for the official legislation of the Church to defend the right of Christians to engage in secular affairs and to participate in public life. Unfortunately, there are nations and forms of government that do restrict the civil liberties of Christians precisely because they are Christians. The Church does not align itself with any particular culture or political system; it can peacefully co-exist with any government that respects the human rights of its citizens. But when certain basic rights are denied, the Church must be faithful to its mission and come to the defense of those who are victims of injustice.

On the other hand, in those countries in which Christians are free to practice their religion and to enjoy the same civil rights as all other citizens, it is sometimes necessary to remind the laity of their obligation to be actively involved in temporal affairs and public service. In its document on the Church in the modern world, the Second Vatican Council made a statement that deserves careful attention by all lay Christians:

> It is a mistake to think that because we have here no lasting city, but seek the city which is to come, we are entitled to shirk our earthly responsibilities; this is to forget that by our faith we are bound all the more to fulfill these responsibilities according to the vocation of each one. But it is no less mistaken to think that we may immerse ourselves in earthly activities as if these latter were utterly foreign to religion, and religion were nothing more than the fulfillment of acts of worship and the observance of a few moral obligations. The Christian who shirks his temporal duties shirks his duties towards his neighbor, neglects God himself, and endangers his eternal salvation. (GS 43)

Pope John Paul II gave the same teaching in his Apostolic Exhortation on the laity, and with equal emphasis: ''In order to achieve their task directed to the Christian animation of the temporal order, the lay faithful *are never to relinquish their partici- pation in 'public life,'* that is, in the many different economic, social, legislative, administrative and cultural areas, which are intended to promote organically and institutionally the *common good''* (CL 42).

Finally, canon 227 reminds the laity that they are to engage in secular affairs of the temporal order as Christians; that is to say, they must apply Gospel values to their professional and civic activities. To do this they need a rightly formed conscience, and it is here that the priests and bishops have an obligation to provide continuing religious education. Bishops especially, as shepherds of the flock, have a serious obligation to teach and interpret the moral principles which have a bearing on the activities and problems of the temporal order.

However, it is sometimes a rather complicated process to proceed from general moral principles to their application to given circumstances. It is in this area that the educated Christian laity, obedient to the teaching of the Church, play the most important role. Therefore, in its document on the Church in the modern world, the Council advises the laity: "Very often their Christian vision will suggest a certain solution in some given situation. Yet it happens rather frequently, and legitimately so, that some of the faithful, with no less sincerity, will see the problem quite dif- ferently. Now if one or another of the proposed solutions is too easily associated with the message of the Gospel, they ought to remember that in those cases no one is permitted to identify the authority of the Church exclusively with his own opinion. Let them, then, try to guide each other by sincere dialogue in a spirit of mutual charity and with anxious interest above all in the common good'' (GS 43).

> *CANON 229:* Lay people have the duty and the right to acquire the knowledge of Christian teaching which is appropriate to each one's capacity and condition, so that they may be able to live

according to this teaching, to proclaim it and if necessary to defend it, and may be capable of playing their part in the exercise of the apostolate.

They also have the right to acquire that fuller knowledge of the sacred sciences which is taught in ecclesiastical universities or faculties or in institutes of religious sciences, attending lectures there and acquiring academic degrees.

Likewise, assuming that the provisions concerning the requisite suitability have been observed, they are capable of receiving from the lawful ecclesiastical authority a mandate to teach the sacred sciences.

We have already seen in canon 217 that all the faithful without exception "have the right to a Christian education, which genuinely teaches them to strive for the maturity of the human person and at the same time to know and live the mystery of salvation." Then, in canon 218, we saw that those who are engaged in fields of sacred study have a just freedom to research matters in which they are expert and to express themselves prudently concerning them, "with due allegiance to the *magisterium* of the Church." The present canon, however, touches on the role of the laity in the ministry of the word (preaching and teaching), which in times past was the domain of the clergy, and especially of the bishop. It is not a question here of the right and the duty of all the Christian faithful to obtain the education necessary for attaining Christian maturity; rather, it is a question of the apostolic use of the knowledge acquired.

Hence, all the faithful have the right to a religious education in accordance with their capability and their condition of life. For some, this may be a rather rudimentary knowledge of the faith, but for others it may be necessary to obtain a much deeper and more specialized formation. Thus, a Catholic physician or politician needs a much deeper grounding in the theological principles that apply to their expertise than does a worker in a factory or a man who tills the soil. In either case, the purpose of such a religious education is to be able to live according to Catholic teaching, to proclaim and defend Catholic teaching, and to participate to some extent in the ministry of the word. If any defense were needed, it is on these grounds that we can justify the existence of Catholic universities that provide professional training in accordance with Gospel values.

What is new in the present legislation, however is the admission of lay students into ecclesiastical faculties and pontifical universities. For centuries, with few exceptions, the pontifical faculties and universities were populated by priests and seminarians. But even before the revised *Code of Canon Law* was promulgated, the Fathers of the Second Vatican Council stated in their document on the Church in the modern world: "It is to be hoped that more of the laity will receive adequate theological formation and that some among them will dedicate themselves professionally to these studies and contribute to their advancement. But for the proper exercise of this role, the faithful, both clerical and lay, should be accorded a lawful freedom of inquiry, of thought and of expression, tempered by humility and courage, in whatever branch of study they have specialized" (GS 62).

There have always been some outstanding laymen who dedicated their lives to the study of sacred doctrine — we think of Gilson and Maritain — but they have been the exception. Since the close of Vatican Council II, however, pontifical universities and faculties that specialize in the sacred sciences have opened their doors to all qualified persons who may wish to work toward ecclesiastical degrees. And once a lay man or woman has earned the required academic degree, it follows logically and justly that they should be capable of receiving the ecclesiastical mandate to teach in pontifical universities or major seminaries. If the Church has taken the first step in admitting the laity to advanced theological studies, then it must take the second step and allow qualified lay persons to teach in those institutions.

But certain questions arise at this point. What subjects are included under the title "sacred sciences"? Should a non-Catholic, an atheist or a Catholic professor who dissents from the teaching of the magisterium be authorized to teach the sacred sciences? To what extent should lay men or women be admitted to the administration and internal activities of a pontifical university or major seminary? Are all the faculties of a pontifical Catholic university under the jurisdiction of the Holy See? Do all professors in a pontifical institution need a mandate from ecclesiastical authority, regardless of the subject taught?

In attempting to answer these questions, we should note first of all that the law of the Church treats of Catholic education in canons 793 and 821. As regards Catholic elementary and secondary schools, they are under the control of the competent ecclesiastical authority, for example, a bishop, a parish priest, a diocesan board of education or a religious institute. Canon 803 states that "formation and education in a Catholic school must be based on the principles of Catholic doctrine, and the teachers must be outstanding in true doctrine and uprightness of life." Then we read in canons 804 and 805 that the bishop is to take care that "those who are appointed as teachers of religion in schools, even non-Catholic ones, are outstanding in true doctrine, in the witness of their Christian life, and in their teaching ability"; but "if religious or moral considerations require it, the bishop has the right to remove them or to demand that they be removed."

When it is a question of higher education — universities, major seminaries and pontifical faculties — a distinction is in order. What we normally refer to when speaking of a Catholic college or university is an institution of higher learning that has been established with the consent of the bishop and is governed by its own particular statutes. However, since canons 215 and 216 authorize the faithful to form their own associations and to promote apostolic action on their own initiative, there is no reason why the laity could not establish universities or centers of higher learning on their own initiative. True, to call such institutions "Catholic" would require the approval of competent ecclesiastical authority, and if any of the sacred sciences were to be taught, the bishop would have to exercise some degree of vigilance. Nevertheless, a university could be a "Catholic" university without being a Church-sponsored university. The reason given by Alvaro del Portillo of Opus Dei is that "the Catholic character of a university is not determined by any dependence on the ecclesiastical hierarchy; the decisive factor is that it should have, and by its scientific work contribute to, a concept of the world inspired by the Catholic faith" (*Faithful and Laity in the Church*, p. 138).

If, however, a university is under ecclesiastical authority, Canon 811 states that "the competent authority is to ensure that in Catholic universities there is established a faculty or an institute or at least a chair of theology" and "in every Catholic university there are to be lectures which principally treat of those theological questions connected with the studies of each faculty." This means that in schools of medicine, law, commerce, etc., there should be courses that treat of theological questions related to their area of specialization. Moreover, canon 810 states that "it is the duty of competent statutory authority to ensure that there be appointed teachers who are not only qualified in scientific and pedagogical expertise, but are also outstanding in their integrity of doctrine and uprightness of life. If these requirements are found to be lacking, it is also that authority's duty to see to it that these teachers are removed from office, in accordance with the procedure determined in the statutes." Finally, canon 812 requires that all "who teach theological subjects in an institute of higher studies must have a mandate from the competent ecclesiastical authority." The foregoing canons are taken almost literally from the Vatican II document on Catholic education (1965).

The legislation of the Church regarding colleges and universities is concerned exclusively with providing a sound religious education for students in Catholic institutions. And since the number of lay men and women specializing in the sacred sciences is increasing yearly, there is also an increasing need for institutes of higher studies where the laity can pursue the academic degrees needed for teaching the sacred sciences. In conjunction with this, the Catholic universities are faced with the problem of providing sufficient remuneration for the services of lay people whose financial needs are usually much greater than those of the celibate clergy or of religious.

Apart from the teaching of the sacred sciences, lay men and women who are professionally competent and well trained in the so-called profane subjects can make a valuable contribution to Catholic higher education. We could almost say that those subjects are more properly the area of expertise for the laity, and that we would expect that the clergy and the religious would make the teaching of the sacred sciences their priority. However, it does not seem likely that it will ever be possible to make such a neat division as to allocate to the clergy and religious all religious and theological teaching, and to the laity all the profane subjects. Nor would such a distribution even be desirable, given the fact that some individuals, whether clergy or laity, are much more competent and better prepared than others to teach a given subject.

Coming now to the strictly ecclesiastical faculties and universities (canons 815-821), the first thing to be noted is that these are institutes dedicated to the study of the sacred sciences and of subjects related to them; furthermore, they are established by the Holy See or with its approval. Only these institutes, which are usually called "pontifical," are authorized to confer academic degrees that have canonical recognition in the Church. The persons who enroll in pontifical universities or faculties must be "outstanding in character, intelligence and virtue" (canon 819). Any student — clerical, religious or lay — who has received the required

pontifical degree "is capable of receiving from the lawful ecclesiastical authority a mandate to teach the sacred sciences"
(canon 229). The reason why the professors of sacred sciences
need a mandate is that they do not teach on their own authority but
by virtue of the mission they have received from the Church.
Moreover, before receiving tenure or being promoted to the highest
rank, professors must have a declaration of *nihil obstat* from the
Holy See as well as a doctorate degree.

Major seminaries are also institutes of higher learning but they
are treated in canon law under the title "The Formation of Clerics"
(canons 232 to 264) and not under the section on higher education
(canons 807 to 821). For our purposes it suffices to note that lay
men and women who fulfill the requirements for teaching in a
major seminary — persons of outstanding virtue and possessing
either the doctorate or the licentiate from a pontifical university or
faculty — may receive from the bishop the mandate to teach. The
determining factor here, however, should not be "equal opportunity" for laity and clergy or for men and women, but the competence
of the individual professor. Nor should the admission of lay men
and women to seminary faculties reach such a point that the
administration of the seminary is for all practical purposes in the
hands of the laity. By the same token, to admit lay students to the
seminary who are not studying for the priesthood would turn the
seminary into a co-educational college or university and thus
destroy the identity of the seminary.

After the Second Vatican Council it became quite common to
argue that seminarians should not be so completely cut off from
daily contact with other lay men and women, and that opinion was
quite defensible in the days when seminarians from their early teen
years until ordination lived a quasi-cloistered life. In many
countries today, however, candidates for the priesthood begin their
studies and formation much later and consequently they are more
mature; they have passed through the turbulent years of adolescence and many of them are college graduates or they have had

experience in the work place. Consequently, as candidates for the priesthood they usually appreciate the discipline of seminary life and the concentration on studies.

> *CANON 228:* Lay people who are found to be suitable are capable of being admitted by the sacred Pastors to those ecclesiastical offices and functions which, in accordance with the provisions of law, they can discharge.
>
> Lay people who are outstanding in the requisite knowledge, prudence and integrity, are capable of being experts or advisors, even in councils in accordance with the law, in order to provide assistance to the Pastors of the Church.

There is really no need to comment on the possible role of expert lay men and women as advisors to the hierarchy. It is simply a matter of common sense and prudence for the clergy to seek the advice of others in matters in which they themselves have no expertise. As regards the admission of lay men and women to certain ecclesiastical offices and functions, that was already foreseen by the Fathers of Vatican Council II who stated in their document on the Church that bishops and priests should willingly heed the prudent advice of the laity and assign duties to them in the service of the Church. This has already been implemented in many dioceses throughout the world. However, we are not speaking here of a strict right of the laity, because the canon says only that the laity are "capable of being admitted" to certain offices and functions. The reason for wording the canon this way is that the functions and offices referred to are either connected with the sacrament of holy orders or have traditionally been assigned to the clergy. Pope John Paul II, in his Apostolic Exhortation on the laity, put it this way:

The Church's mission of salvation in the world is realized not only by the ministers in virtue of the Sacrament of Orders but also by all the lay faithful; indeed, because of their baptismal state and their specific vocation, in the measure proper to each person, the lay faithful participate in the priestly, prophetic and kingly mission of Christ.

The Pastors, therefore, ought to acknowledge and foster the ministries, the offices and roles of the lay faithful that find their *foundation in the Sacraments of Baptism and Confirmation*, indeed, for a good many of them, *in the Sacrament of Matrimony*.

When necessity and expediency in the Church require it, the Pastors, according to established norms from universal law, can entrust to the lay faithful certain offices and roles that are connected to their pastoral ministry but do not require the character of Orders. . . . However, *the exercise of such tasks does not make Pastors of the lay faithful*; in fact, a person is not a minister simply in performing a task, but through sacramental ordination. Only the Sacrament of Orders gives the ordained minister a particular participation in the office of Christ, the Shepherd and Head, and in his Eternal Priesthood. The task exercised in virtue of supply takes its legitimacy formally and immediately from the official deputation given by the Pastors, as well as from its concrete exercise under the guidance of ecclesiastical authority. (CL 23)

From the time of the Middle Ages the Church has frequently suffered from the unlawful intervention of kings, feudal lords and governments, either to confiscate Church property or to control the selection of bishops. The Church necessarily became defensive in protecting itself against such illegal encroachments and, as a result, placed in the hands of the hierarchy many functions that could have been just as easily — and sometimes better — performed by the laity. Today, with clearly established lines between Church and civil authority, the Church can safely confer on lay men and women many of the offices and functions that do not require the sacrament of holy orders. Clearly, any person admitted to ecclesiastical offices and functions should have the requisite qualities: sufficient knowledge or expertise, prudence, and uprightness of life.

But what are the offices and functions that can be assigned to the laity? If they are ecclesiastical in nature, then, as Pope John Paul has stated, they will be conferred by the proper ecclesiastical authority, and in practice this will be either the bishop or the parish priest. The Church is governed by the hierarchy and no matter how intimately the laity are involved in the administration and activities of the diocese or parish, the ultimate authority and responsibility remains with the hierarchy.

The power of government belongs to the Church by divine institution, and those who are in holy orders are capable of exercising it. The laity, however, "can cooperate in this same power in accordance with the law" (canon 129). It is further stated in canon 274 that only the clergy can hold offices in the Church "that require the power of order or the power of ecclesiastical governance." This would seem at the outset to severely limit any kind of collaboration of the laity with the hierarchy in ecclesiastical offices and functions. Such is not the case, however, because both in law and in practice the laity are capable of holding any number of offices in the Church. For example, a qualified lay person may be named to any of the following offices: chancellor of a diocese; finance officer; censor of books; assessor, auditor, defender of the marriage bond, or promoter of justice in a diocesan tribunal; or other offices that can be established at the diocesan or parish level; for example, diocesan or parish director of music or liturgy; director of religious education; director of Catholic charities or editor of the diocesan newspaper.

Another possibility for greater lay involvement is at the parish level, although memories of the abuses of the "trustee system" may prevent many ecclesiastical authorities from even considering the possibility. Nevertheless, Alvaro del Portillo of Opus Dei makes a strong case for the financial control of a parish by the laity:

> It must be realized that nowadays it is not sufficient to have certain moral virtues — prudence or justice — together with a natural talent for finance: one must have technical knowledge of the type normally possessed by those lay people who are trained in finance and economics. Generally speaking, it would be a great waste of energy they fully need for their pastoral duties to expect clerics to obtain such training in sufficient numbers. . . . To grant the laity powers connected with the administration of Church property cannot mean simply giving them a mandate or a canonical mission to act *in place of* clerics on certain bodies or in organizations set up with this in mind. It is not a question of substituting laymen for clerics, although this also may be done; basically it is a question of organizing the Church property in such a way that lay people may administer it *in a natural way* . . . .
>
> A parish is not a community of lay people over which and above which a parish priest exercises the function of caring for souls, but a community made up of members of the faithful — lay and clerical — each of whom has his own particular mission within it. And the property and funds necessary to fulfill the purpose of the parish, from supporting the clergy to carrying out apostolate, may be organized fragmentarily as at present . . . but they might also be organized along different legal lines . . . as property and funds belonging to the parish community. In this case, since all the community would share in the liability, naturally the administrators might be any members of that community, provided they were morally and technically suitable and provided they took appropriate legal precautions, which any society or company would take in such cases. . . . The laity would then be the most appropriate people for this task of administering the

property, either under the parish priest's supervision, or directly under the supervision of the Ordinary by way of competent bodies. (*Faithful and Laity in the Church*, pp. 128-130)

One last note is in order concerning the growing practice and need to admit the laity and lay religious to a sharing in the exercise of pastoral care, whether as associate chaplains to institutions or as pastoral assistants in a parish. Obviously, they can perform only those functions that do not require holy orders, although that leaves a great deal that they can do. According to Church law the official pastor must always be a priest, but in some cases the priest spends a great deal of time and effort on functions and services that do not require holy orders. There is, moreover, the underlying problem of a shortage of priests. Undoubtedly, there must be a more concerted effort to encourage vocations to the priesthood and to "import" priests from nations where vocations are plentiful. In the meantime — and perhaps increasingly in the future — more and more of the laity will be called upon to perform those functions that do not require holy orders but in the past have taken up so much of the priest's time and energy. All this is something quite different from the "non-ordained" ministries and "extraordinary" or special functions that are treated in the following canon.

CANON 230: Lay men whose age and talents meet the requirements prescribed by decree of the Episcopal Conference, can be given the stable ministry of lector and of acolyte, through the prescribed liturgical rite. This conferral of ministry does not, however, give them a right to sustenance or remuneration from the Church.

Lay people can receive a temporary assignment to the role of lector in liturgical actions. Likewise, all lay people can exercise the roles of commentator, cantor, or other such, in accordance with the law.

> Where the needs of the Church require and ministers are not
> available, lay people, even though they are not lectors or aco-
> lytes, can supply certain of their functions, that is, exercise the
> ministry of the word, preside over liturgical prayers, confer
> baptism and distribute Holy Communion, in accordance with the
> provisions of the law.

The first thing to be noted is that the first paragraph of this canon is the only one in this section that makes a distinction between men and women: only men can be admitted to the permanent ministries of lector and acolyte. Secondly, we should recall that canon 150 stipulates that any office that carries with it the full care of souls, for which the order of priesthood is required, cannot be conferred on a person who is not a priest. Finally, according to canon 564 only a priest may be assigned as the chaplain of some community or special group of Christ's faithful; for example, a hospital, a home for the aged, an educational institution, a society or sodality, or a religious community. The reason is that the performance of a chaplain's duties requires holy orders, although persons who are not priests may be assigned as associates or auxiliaries to perform those functions that can be performed by a lay person.

Before the Second Vatican Council the Church conferred the so-called "minor orders" on seminarians as steps toward the priesthood. These minor orders were enumerated as porter, lector, exorcist and acolyte, and they could be conferred only on those who had entered the clerical state with the reception of tonsure. The "major" orders, on the other hand, were listed as subdiaconate, diaconate and priesthood, and the episcopacy was considered to be the fullness of the priesthood. Throughout the centuries there were various and sometimes contradictory opinions offered by theologians as to whether or not both the minor and the major orders were parts of the sacrament of holy orders. There was always a common teaching that the orders of diaconate and priesthood were true sacraments; but as to the subdiaconate and the four minor orders, the most one could offer would be a probable opinion. In former times a man became a cleric with the reception of the tonsure but he did not receive the sacrament of holy orders until he was ordained a deacon. But since Pope Paul VI revised the various ministries in 1972, one enters the clerical state with ordination to the diaconate.

If we speak of a sacrament as any sensible sign or symbol that can serve as a channel of grace to the one who receives it, then we can include many things under the word "sacrament." But if we mean by sacrament a sensible sign, *instituted by Christ*, to confer grace on the one who receives it, then it would be difficult to prove that the subdiaconate and the "minor orders" were truly part of the sacrament of holy orders. In the early Church only bishops, priests and deacons were said to be in the "holy order." Then, as the Church expanded and there was a need to distribute offices and functions more widely, the Church instituted what became known as the "minor" orders that were conferred on clerics who were not priests or deacons. The Church had power and authority to do this because only two of the sacraments — baptism and the Eucharist — were specified by Christ as to matter and form; it was left to the Church to make specific determinations regarding the other sacraments.

What the Church has done in the past, the Church can do — and did do — in the present. In its document on the sacred liturgy (1963), the Second Vatican Council suggested that, in places where no priest is available, Bible services should be conducted by a deacon or by some other person appointed by the bishop. Then, in 1964, the Council established by Pope Paul VI for implementing the liturgical reform described in greater detail the nature and format of the Bible service:

> The structure of the Bible service is to be the same as that of the
> liturgy of the Word at Mass: the Epistle and Gospel of the day's
> Mass are generally read in the vernacular; chants, especially

from the psalms, being sung at the beginning of the service and during it. The person who presides should preach, if he is a deacon; if he is not a deacon, he should read a homily chosen by the bishop or the parish priest. The service should terminate with "the community prayer" or the "prayer of the faithful," and the Lord's prayer. (IO 37)

Notice that the instruction states that if there is no deacon present to preach the homily, the presiding lay person is to "read a homily chosen by the bishop or the parish priest." Only a priest or deacon may preach the homily during a Bible Service or at Mass (canon 767); a lay person "may be allowed to preach in a church or oratory if in certain circumstances it is necessary, or in particular cases would be advantageous, according to the provisions of the Episcopal Conference" (canon 766).

In 1972, Pope Paul VI promulgated a document under the title *Ministeria Quaedam* which is of great significance for the participation of the laity in the liturgical life of the Church. It is, in fact, a revolutionary document, although it is not necessarily the last word on this matter. In fact, some of the bishops who participated in the 1987 Synod on the Laity requested that the document issued by Pope Paul VI should be reconsidered. Responding to this request, Pope John Paul II has set up a commission to study the matter and at this writing we are awaiting the results of their study. In the meantime, however, Pope John Paul II has recommended that the local churches should respect "the essential difference between the ministerial priesthood and the common priesthood, and the difference between the ministries derived from the Sacrament of Orders and those derived from the Sacraments of Baptism and Confirmation" (CL 23).

The canon that we are discussing (canon 230) is based on the changes made by Pope Paul VI in 1972. He abolished the subdiaconate in the Latin Church and allowed lay men to become permanent lectors and acolytes. Moreover, when there is a true need, both men and women may be permitted to perform certain liturgical functions as "extraordinary" or special ministers. The canon summarizes the various liturgical functions that lay people can perform, either because they are men who have received the permanent ministry as acolytes or lectors, or because necessity requires that lay men and/or women supply for the lack of clergy.

Since the former "minor orders" are no longer functions reserved exclusively to the clergy, they are "lay ministries." Nevertheless, the law of the Church at the present time insists that, except for men who have been installed as lectors or acolytes, all other lay persons who perform liturgical functions do so "by invitation" and not by right. It has not yet been clarified whether the capacity of the laity to be invited to perform certain liturgical functions flows from their common priesthood as baptized Christians or whether the services of the laity can be dispensed with whenever sufficient clergy are available. Pope John Paul II expressed his sentiments as follows in his Apostolic Exhortation on the vocation and mission of the laity:

> Following the liturgical renewal promoted by the Council, the lay faithful themselves have acquired a more lively awareness of the tasks that they fulfill in the liturgical assembly and its preparation, and have become more widely disposed to fulfill them: the liturgical celebration, in fact, is a sacred action not simply of the clergy, but of the entire assembly. It is, therefore, natural that the tasks not proper to the ordained ministers be fulfilled by the lay faithful. In this way there is a natural transition from an effective involvement of the lay faithful in the liturgical action to that of announcing the word of God and pastoral care.

> In the same Synod Assembly, however, a critical judgment was voiced along with these positive elements, about a too-indiscriminate use of the word "ministry," the confusion and the equating of the common priesthood and the ministerial

priesthood, the lack of observance of ecclesiastical laws and
norms, the arbitrary interpretation of the concept of "supply,"
the tendency towards a "clericalization" of the lay faithful and
the risk of creating, in reality, an ecclesial structure of parallel
service to that founded on the Sacrament of Orders. . . .

In the first place, then, it is necessary that in acknowledging and
in conferring various ministries, offices and roles on the lay
faithful, the Pastors exercise the maximum care to institute them
on the basis of Baptism, in which these tasks are rooted. It is also
necessary that Pastors guard against a facile yet abusive recourse
to a presumed "situation of emergency" or to "supply by
necessity," where objectively this does not exist or where alternative possibilities could exist through better pastoral
planning.

The various ministries, offices and roles that the lay faithful can
legitimately fulfill in the liturgy, in the transmission of the faith,
and in the pastoral structure of the Church, ought to be exercised
in conformity to their specific lay vocation, which is different
from that of the sacred ministry. (CL 23)

Since the Holy Father referred to the "lack of observance of
ecclesiastical laws and norms" as one of the causes of the confusion and excesses in the admission of the laity to liturgical
functions and sacred ministries, it is important for us to understand
clearly the legislation of the Church on this matter.

The various ministries mentioned in canon 230 are no longer
functions that are reserved to the clergy; they are in fact "ministries
of the laity" or "ministries of the non-ordained." For seminarians,
of course, they still constitute the steps toward the diaconate and
priesthood, but seminarians are not members of the clergy until
they become deacons. Moreover, any man — married or single —
who is ordained a *permanent* deacon is by that very fact a member
of the clergy. That is why there is no mention of permanent deacons
in this section of the *Code of Canon Law*; they are no longer lay
members of the Church although they live "in the world" and are

almost totally involved in secular affairs. With their ordination to the diaconate, they have been admitted to holy orders and therefore have all the rights and duties that pertain to the sacred ministry of deacons. They are not, therefore, individuals who function as "extraordinary ministers" in cases of need or when there is a short supply of priests.

Only time will tell whether or not the permanent diaconate really serves the best interest of the Church in all parts of the world. In mission countries or in areas in which the Church is only recently established, the permanent deacons may well be a necessity, due to the shortage of priests. On the other hand, in many dioceses of the First World the permanent diaconate may prove to be a contributing factor to the decrease in vocations to the priesthood.

Returning to the participation of the laity in sacred ministries, we note that canon 230 allows for men who meet the requirements established by the Conference of Bishops to be admitted to the permanent ministry of lector and acolyte. According to Pope Paul VI, who made these profound changes, the restriction on the permanent ministry of lector and acolyte to men is in accordance with "the venerable tradition of the Church." But what are the functions of the permanent lector and permanent acolyte? The lector is officially delegated to read the word of God in the liturgical assembly; his ministry is, therefore, the "ministry of the Word." His specific duties are to read the Sacred Scripture in the liturgy, except the Gospel, which is restricted to deacons and priests; to read the Passion in Holy Week, but possibly to reserve the words of Christ to a priest or deacon; to read the psalm between the readings at Mass; to read the petitions of the Prayer of the Faithful when a deacon or cantor is not available; to direct the music and the lay participation in the liturgy, unless there is a designated music director. In addition, the lector is authorized to teach catechism and to prepare individuals for the reception of the sacraments; to supervise those who are delegated to do the liturgical readings on a temporary basis; to give instructions to those who are as yet ignorant of the faith. As is evident, some of the functions indicated are by way of "supply" when the proper persons are not available; but the distinctive functions of the lector are catechesis and evangelization. Furthermore, these are ministries that are common to all of Christ's faithful, both men and women, since they have· their foundation in the sacraments of baptism and confirmation.

Perhaps most people will think of the lector exclusively as a lay person who is deputed to do the public readings in the liturgical assembly. However, there is another much more important function of the lector: catechesis with a view to evangelization. Indeed, by reason of their status as baptized Christians, any lay man or woman can be trained and then officially deputed to function publicly as a catechist. The apostolic task of catechesis is much more than instructing children in the catechism or engaging in a purely academic form of teaching religion; it is more closely related to preaching, because its aim is to "develop in individuals a living, explicit and active faith, enlightened by doctrine." That is the description given in the Vatican II document on the pastoral office of bishops. In his excellent little book on the laity, Alvaro del Portillo says: "To be a catechist is not the same thing as to teach religious knowledge in a school. To confuse these two activities, as is sometimes done, is to undervalue the catechistic function. A teacher of religion might well maintain a cold academic attitude in his work, while a catechist is always an apostle. The objective goal . . . of a teacher of religious education is to transmit certain facts; a catechist's goal is to form in his hearers a living, explicit and active faith" (*Faithful and Laity in the Church*, p. 141).

The ministry of the acolyte is a "ministry of the altar," since his function is to assist the deacon in ministering to the priest. His functions are to prepare the altar and the sacred vessels for the celebration of the liturgy; to assist the deacon and the celebrant of the Mass; to supervise any others who may be temporarily assisting at the liturgy (e.g., the altar boys); to purify the sacred vessels after

Communion (functions which formerly belonged to deacons or subdeacons). In addition to the foregoing "ordinary" functions, there are certain "extraordinary" ministries that can be performed by the permanent acolyte, but only in cases of necessity. For example, when a deacon or priest is not available or in case of the large number of communicants, the acolyte may distribute Holy Communion. He may also, when necessary, bring Holy Communion to the sick. There are various documents issued by the Vatican that treat of certain aspects of the acolyte's role in giving Communion, but these will be of interest only to bishops, pastors or the permanent acolytes themselves. Another "extraordinary" function of the acolyte is to expose the Blessed Sacrament for veneration by the people and then to repose the Sacred Host, if no priest or deacon is available, but he is not authorized to give the blessing with the monstrance.

At this point one may logically ask why the Church law, after referring to permanent installation as lector or acolyte, states in the very next paragraph that any lay person — man or woman — may receive a "temporary assignment" to function as lector in liturgical actions and may also exercise the role of cantor, commentator and such like. Even more, the third paragraph states that "where the needs of the Church require and ministers are not available," a lay person — again, man or woman — can supply the sacred functions that would otherwise be performed by a lector or acolyte. Consequently, under certain conditions men or women who have not been installed as lectors or acolytes may nevertheless officially exercise the ministry of the word, lead public liturgical prayers, confer baptism in case of necessity and even distribute Holy Communion. Very likely it is this third paragraph that caught the attention of bishops and parish priests and has led to certain excesses referred to by Pope John Paul II.

CANON 231:   Lay people who are pledged to the special
service of the Church, whether permanently or for a time, have a
duty to acquire the appropriate formation which their role demands, so that they may conscientiously, earnestly and diligently fulfill this role.

Without prejudice to the provisions of canon 230, 1, they have
the right to a worthy remuneration befitting their condition,
whereby, with due regard also to the provisions of the civil law,
they can becomingly provide for their own needs and the needs
of their families. Likewise, they have the right to have their
insurance, social security and medical benefits duly
safeguarded.

It has already been stated in canon 230 that men who are
installed in the permanent ministry of lector or acolyte cannot claim
any remuneration from the Church for their services in these
ministries. The same holds true for all other participation of the
laity in the ministries and functions mentioned in canon 230. The
clergy, of course, since they have dedicated their lives to the sacred
ministry, are entitled to a just remuneration that will provide for the
necessities of life, as is stated in canon 281. However, any lay
person who is employed by Church authorities for some particular
service has a right to receive a salary or fee that is proportionate to
the service rendered and in keeping with his or her state of life.

As more and more lay people hold offices or perform services
for the Church, the financial burdens of dioceses, parishes and
Catholic institutions will become increasingly heavy. In a sense it
is rather paradoxical that in an age of technology that produces so
many labor-saving devices, dioceses, parishes and Catholic institutions are constantly increasing the staff of salaried workers.
This, in turn, results in greater and heavier demands on the ordinary lay faithful. We need but think of the prohibitive cost of
Catholic medical services and Catholic education, which were

formerly staffed almost entirely by men and women religious who lived in community under the vow of poverty. Obviously, when married men and women are employed for the same services, social justice requires that they receive a salary that provides for their legitimate needs in the home and family. But it is also part of social justice to provide the services of the Church without pricing those services beyond the financial resources of the faithful. Perhaps in many areas the Church authorities could cut back on the bureaucracy in dioceses and parishes; and perhaps generous men and women could be encouraged to serve the various institutions of the Church either on a voluntary basis or for a just but more modest salary.

We have now completed our survey of the section of the *Code of Canon Law* that treats of the rights and duties of the laity in the Church. We have noted that in some respects there are inconsistencies that call for further clarification and, as was stated by Pope John Paul II, some of the legislation has been interpreted and applied too loosely. This is especially true in regard to the admission of the laity to the sacred ministries of word and sacrament. In their eagerness to involve the laity in these ministries, some bishops and priests are in reality drawing the laity away from their primary mission, which is in the world. In doing so, they are unwittingly "clericalizing" the laity, with the result, perhaps, that some men who would otherwise have become priests or permanent deacons are content with their lay participation in sacred ministry.

There is, moreover, a special problem as regards the admission of women to the sacred ministries. If, as was decreed by Pope Paul VI, the former minor orders have been reduced to two — lector and acolyte — and if those ministries are now assigned to the laity, then one would expect that both women and men could be admitted to those ministries. And if the reason for excluding women is that the functions of acolyte are closely related to the priesthood and holy orders, which is reserved for men, then why is it that a woman may be allowed to distribute Holy Communion in case of necessity? And, further, if a woman can under specified conditions be an extraordinary minister of the Eucharist, why could not her daughter supply as an altar girl? Perhaps the Church will have to make a choice: either admit both men and women to all the sacred ministries available to the laity or else reserve *all* the functions of acolyte to men and allow women to exercise the functions of lector. It should be noted, however, that as regards the distribution of Holy Communion, this is an extraordinary ministry even for the acolyte.

After treating so extensively of the role of the laity in the ministries of word and sacrament, one may get the impression that lay participation in these ministries is the most important aspect of the mission of the laity in the Church. But that is not the case. Since there is an essential difference between the ministerial or ordained priesthood and the common priesthood of the laity, there should likewise be a difference between the mission of the laity and that of the clergy. What that difference is will be investigated in the following chapter.

CHAPTER 4

APOSTOLATE OF THE LAITY

The topic discussed by the 1987 Synod of Bishops was given the title: ''The Vocation and Mission of the Laity in the Church and in the World Twenty Years after the Second Vatican Council.'' The very wording of the title implies that the concepts of vocation and mission are two distinct realities, although they are intimately interrelated. Some persons, however, use the terms interchangeably because they see the vocation of the laity as a calling to permeate the secular or temporal order with Christian values and the spirit of the Gospel. And this, they say, is the same as describing the mission of the laity.

Although it is true to say — as the Second Vatican Council already did say in various documents — that all the Christian faithful, including the laity, are called to some form of apostolic activity and evangelization, the apostolate is not the only element in the Christian vocation. To identify the vocation of the laity with their mission or apostolate is to speak in a purely functional manner that leads to what Pope Pius XII called ''the heresy of action.'' Vocation is a broader concept than apostolate or mission because the vocation or calling of every Christian is first and above all to strive for the perfection of charity, as Christ taught: to love the Lord their God with all their heart and mind and strength and secondly, to love their neighbor and to express this love through the corporal or spiritual works of mercy. Hence, in its document on the Church, the Second Vatican Council described the fundamental and primary vocation of the People of God as follows: "All the faithful, whatever their condition or state — though each in his own way — are called by the Lord to that perfection of sanctity by which the Father himself is perfect." Therefore, the vocation to mission or apostolate should flow from one's vocation to holiness, as is stated in the Vatican II document on the laity: "The apostolate of the laity derives from their very Christian vocation" (AA 1).

However, although the terms "vocation" and "apostolate" are not interchangeable, they are closely related because, as we have said, love and service for one's neighbor should flow from one's love of God. This is implied in the teaching of Christ when he said that whatever was done for the least of his little ones was done for him, and when he commanded his apostles to love one another "as I loved you." Conversely, it is through the performance of their ordinary daily tasks that the faithful can most effectively strive for the perfection of charity and increase the intimacy of their union with God. The reason for this is that in the exercise of virtue through the spiritual and corporal works of mercy an individual can become better disposed for the practice of prayer and a more contemplative attitude. Such was the teaching of St. Gregory the Great: "The active life precedes the contemplative life in time, because from good works one is led to contemplation." But then, from the practice of prayer and the more contemplative activities, one is better disposed to give to others "the fruits of contemplation" in the apostolate.

The laity, therefore, have a definite role to play in the overall mission of the Church. And in looking again at the document on the laity issued by the Second Vatican Council, we find a clear statement on the mission of lay Christians:

> In the Church there is diversity of ministry but unity of mission. To the apostles and their successors Christ has entrusted the office of teaching, sanctifying and governing in his name and by

his power. But the laity are made to share in the priestly, prophetical and kingly office of Christ; they have, therefore, in the Church and in the world, their own assignment in the mission of the whole People of God. In the concrete, their apostolate is exercised when they work at the evangelization and sanctification of men; it is exercised, too, when they endeavor to have the Gospel spirit permeate and improve the temporal order, going about it in a way that bears clear witness to Christ and helps forward the salvation of men. The characteristic of the lay state being a life led in the midst of the world and of secular affairs, laymen are called by God to make of their apostolate, through the vigor of their Christian spirit, a leaven in the world. (AA 2)

The mission of the laity is the same as the mission of the Church, namely, to bring the Gospel message to all nations and thus lead all people to salvation in Christ. But, we repeat, not all of the faithful perform the same functions in that general mission of the Church. Indeed, the laity will normally have much greater freedom of choice than do priests and religious in determining how and where they will participate actively in the Church's mission. Priests, because of their promise of obedience to the bishop, and religious, because of their vow to live according to their particular rule of life, have an obligation to dedicate themselves to those ministries and functions that flow from holy orders or religious profession. That leaves a vast area of apostolate that is properly the domain of the laity. It is interesting to note that as early as 1945 Monsignor J. Escrivá, the founder of Opus Dei was speaking of these matters and that his teaching is echoed in the documents of the Second Vatican Council:

We must consider, but not confuse, two fundamental notions: first, the notion of state, which distinguishes the priest from the simple member of the faithful; and second, the vocation to holiness, common to all Christians.

The clerical state is characterized by a number of duties imposed by the priest's specific mission in the service of God, for he is called, by reason of the sacrament of orders which he has received, to help his brothers with the services proper to his *ministerium verbi et sacramentorum*, his preaching and his administration of the sacraments.

The lay state also has a character which is proper to itself; this takes the form of the ministry peculiar to lay people within the Mystical Body of Christ: they must assume personal responsibility in the professional and social order, so as to imbue all earthly realities with a Christian spirit, *so that in all things God may be glorified through Jesus Christ* (1 P 4:11). (*Conversations with Msgr. Josemaría Escrivá*, Dublin, 1968.)

APOSTOLATE OR MINISTRY?

Before we can discuss in greater detail the various activities that are proper to the laity, it is necessary to clarify the meaning of the words "apostolate" and "ministry." Prior to the Second Vatican Council, and especially through the efforts of St. Vincent Pallotti (1850) and the vigorous endorsement of Catholic Action by Pope Pius IX (1878) and his successors, the word "apostolate" had a much wider meaning than the word "ministry." For all practical purposes the latter term always signified the sacred ministry of word and sacrament that was restricted to those in holy orders; and the laity were the passive recipients of that ministry. But as the laity were encouraged more and more, and especially by Pope Pius XII (1958), to enroll in the ranks of Catholic Action, it became necessary to define more precisely the role of the laity in the mission of the Church and to give a name to their activity.

Pope Pius XI (1939) had described Catholic Action as "the participation of the laity in the hierarchical apostolate of the Church." Then the question was raised: To what extent can the laity participate in the hierarchical apostolate? Pope Leo XIII (1903) had stated that the authority to preach and to teach belongs to the bishops, though they may delegate it to priests. The laity may not receive this delegation, although if they have the intelligence and the competence, they may pass on to others what they have received, and thus echo the teaching of the masters. "To resist the will of the bishops," said Pope Leo XIII, "and to wish to teach them rather than to listen to them, is quite contrary to the duty of laymen. It is no less contrary to that of the clergy, who have only to remember the oath of obedience which each of them made to his bishop on the day of his ordination" (cf. "The Lay Apostolate," in *Papal Teaching*, St. Paul Editions, 1960).

Later, during the pontificate of Pope Pius XII, the meaning of apostolate, and particularly of the lay apostolate, was still being discussed. Thus, in an address to the World Congress of the Lay Apostolate in 1951, the Holy Father tended to restrict the apostolate to those functions and services that are truly a participation in the hierarchical apostolate. It is in that context that he posed a series of questions:

> Can we say that everyone is called to the apostolate in the strict sense of the word? God has not given to everyone either the possibility or the aptitude. One can hardly ask a wife and mother, who has to look after the Christian upbringing of her children and has to work at home, besides helping her husband to feed their little ones, to do apostolic work of this kind. The vocation to be an apostle is therefore not addressed to all alike.
>
> It is certainly not easy to draw an exact line of demarcation, showing precisely where the true apostolate of the laity begins. Should it include, for example, the education given by the mother of a family, or by the men and women teachers engaged with holy zeal in the practice of their professions? Or the conduct of a reputable and openly Catholic doctor whose conscience never wavers when there is a question of the natural and divine

law and who fights with all his might in defense of the Christian
dignity of married persons and the sacred rights of their offspring? Should it include even the action of a Catholic statesman
who sponsors a generous housing policy in favor of the less
fortunate?

Many would be inclined to answer in the negative, seeing in all
these examples merely the accomplishment, very laudable in
itself but obligatory, of the duties of one's state.

Today, however, after the numerous declarations of the Second Vatican Council on the role of the laity in the Church and in the
world, the answers to the questions posed by Pope Pius XII in 1951
would be quite different. Indeed, as early as 1932 the founder of
Opus Dei, Monsignor Escrivá, was calling for a rejection of the
definition of lay apostolate as a participation in the hierarchical
apostolate. "There is no reason," he said, "why the secular
apostolate should always be a mere participation in the apostolate
of the hierarchy. Secular people too have to have a duty to do
apostolate, not because they have received a canonical mission, but
because they are part of the Church" (*Conversations*).

No longer do we speak of the lay apostolate as a participation
in the mission of the Church that is completely under the control of
the hierarchy. The laity have a certain freedom and autonomy
within the secular sphere of apostolic activity; indeed, in some
matters they may be governed more by civil law than by ecclesiastical authority. And now that the lay apostolate is no longer defined
as a sharing in the hierarchical apostolate, it is possible to describe
the apostolate of the laity in much broader terms than those used by
Pope Pius XII. This wider definition of apostolate is found in the
Vatican II document on the laity:

The Church was founded to spread the kingdom of Christ over all
the earth for the glory of God the Father, to make all men
partakers in redemption and salvation, and through them to

establish the right relationship of the entire world to Christ.
Every activity of the Mystical Body with this in view goes by the
name of "apostolate"; the Church exercises it through all its
members, though in various ways. (AA 2)

In accordance with the teaching of the Second Vatican
Council, we have stated repeatedly that the specifically "lay"
apostolate is the sanctification of the world and the temporal order
through the conscientious performance of the duties of their state in
life or particular condition. Moreover, the Council frequently
reminds the laity not to neglect their Christian and apostolic duties
in the secular sphere under the false assumption that one's involvement in temporal affairs, such as political, social, or economic
activities, can be completely divorced from religion and morality.
Much less is a Christian permitted to make such a separation
between Church and State that he or she would justify an action that
is legal according to civil law but is in fact a violation of the law of
God or of human rights.

We have seen that the apostolate is now defined as any activity
that promotes the mission that Christ gave to all the members of the
Church: the redemption and sanctification of all mankind. We have
also emphasized once again that the area of apostolate proper to the
laity is the temporal order. However, since the close of the Second
Vatican Council the laity have also been admitted, under certain
conditions, to some ministries in the Church that were formerly
reserved to the clergy. Thus, Pope Paul VI stated that "together
with the ordained ministries, whereby certain people are appointed
pastors and consecrate themselves in a special way to the service of
the community, the Church recognizes the place of non-ordained
ministries which can offer a particular service to the Church." As a
result, it has become quite common for some persons to prefer to
speak of the "ministry of the laity" rather than "apostolate of the
laity," or to use these expressions interchangeably. In fact, there
is sometimes a tendency to replace the word "apostolate" with

other words such as "vocation," "mission," "ministry," "function," or "pastoral activity." Pope John Paul II took note of this in his Apostolic Exhortation on the Synod on the Laity:

> The ministries which exist and are at work at this time in the Church are all, even in their variety of forms, a participation in Jesus Christ's own ministry as the Good Shepherd. . . .
>
> In a primary position in the Church are the *ordained ministries,* that is, the ministries *that come from the Sacrament of Orders.* . . . The mission of the Apostles, which the Lord Jesus continues to entrust to the Pastors of his people, is a true service, significantly referred to in Sacred Scripture as "*diakonia,*" namely, service or ministry. . . .
>
> When necessity and expediency in the Church require it, the Pastors, according to established norms from universal law, can entrust to the lay faithful certain offices and roles that are connected to their pastoral ministry but do not require the character of Orders. . . . However, *the exercise of such tasks does not make Pastors of the lay faithful*; in fact, a person is not a minister simply in performing a task, but through sacramental ordination. Only the Sacrament of Orders gives the ordained minister a particular participation in the office of Christ, the Shepherd and Head, and in his Eternal Priesthood. . . .
>
> The recent Synodal Assembly has provided an extensive and meaningful overview of the situation in the Church on the ministries, offices and roles of the baptized. . . . In the same Synod Assembly, however, a critical judgment was voiced . . . about a too-indiscriminate use of the word "ministry."
>
> Precisely to overcome these dangers the Synod Fathers have insisted on the necessity to express with greater clarity, and with a more precise terminology, both *the unity of the Church's mission* in which all the baptized participate, and the substantial *diversity of the ministry* of Pastors which is rooted in the Sacra-

ment of Orders, all the while respecting the other ministries, offices and roles in the Church, which are rooted in the Sacraments of Baptism and Confirmation. . . .

The various ministries, offices and roles that the lay faithful can legitimately fulfill in the liturgy, in the transmission of the faith, and in the pastoral structure of the Church, ought to be exercised *in conformity to their specific lay vocation*, which is different from that of the sacred ministry. (CL 21)

The foregoing quotation gives us the key to the distinction between apostolate and ministry. Unlike the apostolate, which applies to any activity by which the mission of the Church is promoted, ministry signifies primarily those functions and offices that flow from holy orders or by Church law have been reserved to ordained ministers. Normally we speak of two types of ministry that belong to the clergy: ministry of the word and ministry of the sacraments; that is, preaching and teaching the Gospel message with a canonical mandate from the ecclesiastical authority and administering the sacraments to the faithful. However, some of the tasks or functions performed by the clergy — for example, teaching catechism, giving religious education, leading public prayers or holding certain offices in the parish or diocese — do not necessarily have to be performed by an ordained minister. When, therefore, the laity perform such tasks they are, as Pope John Paul II advocated, performing functions that are "in conformity to their specific lay vocation," a vocation that stems from their baptism and not from holy orders. In fact, the redistribution of ministries since the Second Vatican Council will not only admit lay men and women to functions from which they were formerly excluded, but it may also serve to withdraw the clergy from tasks that properly belong to the laity.

What would be an adequate description of ministry as distinct from apostolate? There is no agreement on this point, and that is one of the reasons why the two terms are being used interchangeably. A few examples, chosen at random, will illustrate the discrepancy among those who have attempted to formulate a definition of ministry.

The Faith and Order Commission of the World Council of Churches stated in *The New Delhi Report*, published in 1962, that ministry is "any kind of service by which a Christian, exercising his particular skill and gift, however humble, helps his fellow Christians or his fellow men in the name of Christ." It should be noted, however, that in the same *Report* the Commission acknowledged that the ordained have a special kind of ministry: "to strengthen and teach, to encourage and unite all the several witnesses in their various callings whose ministry is set in the heart of the secular world's activity."

Yves Congar, O.P., in his *Lay People in the Church* (revised edition, 1965), after a lengthy citation of passages in the New Testament to prove his point, states: "Those energies in Jesus Christ which represent a personal good . . . a good concerned with salvation and fellowship, are communicated to everybody; but the mission and competency to do certain acts for or upon others, the charge of the institutional means to salvation, in a word, the ministry, is communicated only to some and this, moreover, sets them apart from the rest" (p. 170). In other words, salvation and fellowship through the gift of God's grace are offered to each Christian on a personal basis; but the sacred ministry by which the means to salvation and fellowship are brought to individuals has been committed to the ministerial, hierarchical priesthood.

Finally, in his book entitled *Theology of Ministry* (1983), Thomas O'Meara, O.P. describes ministry as follows: "Christian ministry is the public activity of a baptized follower of Jesus Christ flowing from the Spirit's charism and an individual personality on behalf of a Christian community to witness to, serve and realize the kingdom of God" (p. 142).

The Church is still in the process of redistributing the various ministries and as a result the very definition of ministry is subject to change. For the present, however, it is helpful to note that in the document on the laity the Fathers of the Second Vatican Council distinguished between apostolate and ministry: "The apostolate of the Church, and of all its members, is primarily directed to making available to the world through words and deeds, the message of Christ and communicating his grace. This is done principally through the ministry of the word and sacraments, committed in a special way to the clergy, but in which the laity have an important role to fill as 'cooperators in the truth.' In this arrangement most especially the apostolate of the laity and the pastoral ministry complement each other."

We can more readily accept the distinction between apostolate and ministry if we also accept the essential and specific distinction between the ordained, ministerial priesthood and the common priesthood of the laity. Those who are in holy orders share in a very special way in the priestly, prophetic and kingly functions of Christ and for that reason, as was stated by Pope John Paul II, the ministries that flow from holy orders are in a "primary position in the Church." Hence, the ministry of liturgy and sacraments (priestly function), the ministry of the word (prophetic function), and the exercise of power and authority in the Church (kingly function) are functions and offices proper to the clergy; they are "ordained ministries."

When Pope Paul VI abolished certain "minor orders" and retained only the functions of lector and acolyte, he clearly stated that these functions are now to be called "ministries," and they may be committed to the laity. However, we repeat that the role of the laity in the mission of the Church is primarily and normally in the temporal order, and this constitutes the *lay apostolate*, whether performed individually or in a group, and whether carried out with authorization from the hierarchy or with the autonomy that rightly belongs to the laity in the secular order. If, however, certain members of the laity are admitted to specified sacred ministries because of some necessity or emergency, then we may rightly speak of "lay ministries," but meaning that they are ministries precisely because they are a special form of participation in the priestly and prophetic functions of the clergy and, secondly, because they are performed under some sort of canonical mandate or installation by ecclesiastical authority. Thomas O'Meara, O.P., in his book on ministry, has rightly observed the need to restrict the word "ministry" to its proper theological meaning: "We cannot continue a universalist theology of ministry in which every legitimate and moral human enterprise is ministry. . . . Defining ministry narrowly does not produce an elite group of ministers but lets ministry challenge the potential ministry of every baptized person. When all is ministry, ministry fades away" (p. 159).

THE LAY APOSTOLATE

Although, as we have seen in our commentary on canon 230, lay men and women may under certain conditions be invited to perform functions in the sacred ministry, they are usually classified as "extraordinary ministers" when they do so. This means, of course, that the "ordinary" functions of the laity in the Church and in the world are in another area, namely, in the temporal or secular order. This is what constitutes the apostolate of the laity, and in that sphere they enjoy freedom and autonomy. Of course, if the laity participate in the mission of the Church in a public manner and in the name of the Church, then they would necessarily need the approbation of proper ecclesiastical authority. But apart from that, they may freely engage in the lay apostolate either as individuals or as members of some lay association or movement. It is also possible that one or another lay person may be gifted with a special charism for some particular apostolic activity, as was stated by Pope John Paul II in his Apostolic Exhortation following the Synod on the Laity:

The Holy Spirit, while bestowing diverse ministries in Church communion, enriches it still further with particular gifts or promptings of grace, called *charisms.* These can take a great variety of forms, both as a manifestation of the absolute freedom of the Spirit who abundantly supplies them, and as a response to the varied needs of the Church in history. . . .

Whether they be exceptional and great or simple and ordinary, the charisms are *graces of the Holy Spirit that have, directly or indirectly, a usefulness for the ecclesial community,* ordered as they are to the building up of the Church, to the well-being of humanity and to the needs of the world.

Even in our own times there is no lack of a fruitful manifestation of various charisms among the faithful, women and men. These charisms are given to individual persons, and can even be shared by others in such ways as to continue in time a precious and effective heritage, serving as a source of a particular spiritual affinity among persons. . . .

The charisms are *received in gratitude* both on the part of the one who receives them, and also on the part of the entire Church. They are in fact a singularly rich source of grace for the vitality of the apostolate and for the holiness of the whole Body of Christ, provided that they be gifts that come truly from the Spirit and are exercised in full conformity with the authentic promptings of the Spirit. In this sense the *discernment of charisms* is always necessary. . . .

For this reason no charism dispenses a person from reference and submission to the *Pastors of the Church.* (CL 24)

Charisms, as Pope John Paul II indicates, in conformity with the teaching of St. Paul, are always linked to ministry or apostolate. Charisms are not given as a witness to personal holiness nor for the spiritual growth of the individual person; they are given for building up the Body of Christ, the extension of the kingdom of

God and the good of the Christian community. That is why, for example, it is theologically inaccurate to speak of "the charism of celibacy" in the priestly life when defending the Church's discipline that requires an unmarried clergy.

Returning to our discussion of the apostolate that is most properly the apostolate of the laity, we note first of all a statement in the document on the laity from the Second Vatican Council:

> From the fact of their union with Christ, the Head, flows the right and duty of the laity to be apostles. Inserted as they are into the Mystical Body of Christ by baptism and strengthened by the power of the Holy Spirit in confirmation, it is by the Lord himself that they are assigned to the apostolate. . . .
>
> It is the Lord himself . . . who is once more inviting all the laity to unite themselves to him even more intimately, to consider his interests as their own (Ph 2:5) and to join in his mission as Savior. . . . He sends them on the Church's apostolate, an apostolate that is one, yet has different forms and methods; an apostolate that must always be adapting itself to the needs of the moment. (AA 3)

This call of the laity to participate actively in the mission and apostolate of the Church is by no means an innovation of the Second Vatican Council. In an address to the Christian Workers of Belgium in 1949 Pope Pius XII vigorously defended the role of the laity in the apostolate:

> What you are doing ought to be a shattering answer to the slanders of adversaries who accuse the Church of jealously keeping the laity in bondage, without allowing them any personal activity or assigning them any work proper to their condition. That is not her attitude and it never has been. . . . Is it not as ridiculous as it is offensive to accuse the clergy of keeping the laity in a humiliating state of inaction? In family, educational

or social matters, in science or art, literature or the press, radio or cinema, in political campaigns for the election of legislators or the determination of their constitutional powers and duties, a vast and fertile field of action is open to Catholic lay people in every direction.

It is true; we cannot blame the Church or the Church's teaching for the lack of zealous lay apostles. The fault lies either with the laity themselves, who for one reason or another have not lived up to their baptismal commitment; or with the clergy, who have not promoted the lay apostolate by their preaching and teaching or, in some cases, have been unwilling to relinquish those tasks and functions that could be just as easily or even better performed by the laity. We have already discussed at sufficient length the admission of lay Christians to certain sacred functions as extraordinary ministers. We have also recognized the fact that some chosen individuals may be gifted with special charisms for promoting the mission of the Church. Now we want to focus our attention on the areas of apostolate that are the special domain of the laity; but before we do that, it is necessary to clarify certain points concerning the lay apostolate.

When Catholic Action was first organized by Pope Pius XI in 1930, this particular lay apostolate was seen as a form of close collaboration with the hierarchy, but always requiring some sort of mandate from the hierarchy. The laity have always been free to engage in apostolic activity on their own, of course, but even in the present legislation of the Church, canon 216 states that no organization or movement in the Church can call itself Catholic without the approval and authorization of competent ecclesiastical authority. In other words, no one may speak or act in the name of the Church without some kind of official endorsement from the hierarchy. This is the position held by those who maintain that the primary instruments of apostolate and ministry in the Church are the clergy.

There is, however, a vast area for apostolic activity that can best be exercised by the laity and it cannot be done as effectively by others. For that reason the Second Vatican Council repeatedly insisted that the apostolate of the laity is most properly located in the world, amidst temporal realities. There is, of course, a danger of emphasizing the secular to such an extent that one unwittingly cultivates religious indifference and secularism. This can be avoided, however, if one remembers that apostolate by its very definition means bringing the message and values of Christ to the world in the hope of transforming the world. Thus, in his Apostolic Exhortation on the laity Pope John Paul II wrote: "The living and personal Gospel, *Jesus Christ himself, is the 'good news' and the bearer of joy* that the Church announces each day, and to whom the Church bears testimony before all people. The lay faithful have an essential and irreplaceable role in this announcement and in this testimony: through them the Church of Christ is made present in the various sectors of the world, as a sign and source of hope and of love" (CL 7).

In 1980 the American bishops published a pastoral reflection on the role of the laity in the Church, entitled *Called and Gifted*. In the spirit of the Second Vatican Council, they strongly affirmed first of all that the apostolate proper to the laity is a secular one; only after that did they refer to the active participation of the laity in ecclesial ministries.

> The whole Church faces unprecedented situations in the contemporary world, and lay people are at the cutting edge of these new challenges. It is they who engage directly in the tasks of relating Christian values and practices to complex questions such as those of business ethics, political choice, economic security, quality of life, cultural development, and family planning. . . . In those areas of life in which they are uniquely present and with which they have special competency because of their

particular talents, education and experience, they are an extension of the Church's redeeming presence in the world. (USCC, Washington, D.C.)

The foregoing passage faithfully echoes the sentiments expressed by Pope Paul VI in his document on evangelization in the modern world, promulgated in 1975:

> Laymen, whose vocation commits them to the world and to various temporal enterprises, should exercise a special form of evangelization. . . . The special field for their evangelical activity is the wide and complex arena of politics, sociology and economics. They can be effective also in the spheres of culture, the sciences, the arts, international relations and the communication media. There are certain other fields that are especially appropriate for evangelization such as human love, the family, the education of children and adolescents, the practice of the various professions and the relief of human suffering. If laymen who are actively involved in these spheres are inspired with the evangelical spirit, if they are competent and are determined to bring into play all those Christian powers in themselves which so often lie hidden and dormant, then all these activities will be all the more helpful in the building up of the kingdom of God and in bringing salvation in Jesus Christ. (EN 70)

We have stated repeatedly that by reason of their configuration to Christ through baptism, all the members of the Church without exception share in the same vocation to perfection and to an active participation in the mission of the Church. But among the lay faithful the "secular character" of their state in life sets them apart, but without separating them completely from priests and religious, and much less from the Church. For the Church, as Pope Paul VI told members of secular institutes in 1972, "has an authentic secular dimension, inherent to her inner nature and

mission, which is deeply rooted in the mystery of the Word In-
carnate, and which is realized in different forms through her
members."

As a consequence, Pope John Paul II stated in his Apostolic
Exhortation on the laity: "The lay faithful's *position in the Church*,
then, comes to be fundamentally defined by their *newness in
Christian life* and distinguished by their *secular character*" (CL
25).

LAY PARTICIPATION IN THE PARISH

Pope John Paul II reminded the laity that their "participation in the
life of the Church finds its first and necessary expression in the life
and mission of the *particular Church*, in the diocese" (CL 25);
moreover, he added, "the ecclesial community, while always
having a universal dimension, finds its most immediate and visible
expression in the *parish*" (CL 26). As a child is born into the
domestic society of home and family, so also the baptized Christian
is born into the parish community. In fact, the Holy Father refers to
the parish as "*the Church living in the midst of the homes of her
sons and daughters*" (CL 26).

We are accustomed to think of the parish as a specified
territory within the diocese or as a cluster of buildings under the
management of the clergy. It is both of these things, of course,
because canon 515 describes a parish as "a certain community of
Christ's faithful stably established within a particular church,"
meaning a diocese. But speaking theologically, Pope John Paul II
stated: "The parish is not principally a structure, a territory, or a
building. . . . Plainly and simply, the parish is founded on a
theological reality, because it is a *Eucharistic community*. This
means that the parish is a community properly suited for celebrat-
ing the Eucharist, the living source for its upbuilding and the

sacramental bond of its being in full communion with the whole Church'' (CL 26).

In an address to the clergy of Rome in 1963, Pope Paul VI spoke of the contribution the parish can make to the faithful:

> We believe simply that this old and venerable structure of the parish has an indispensable mission of great contemporary importance: to create the basic community of the Christian people; to initiate and gather the people in the accustomed expression of liturgical life; to conserve and renew the faith in the people of today; to serve as the school for teaching the salvific message of Christ; to put solidarity in practice and work the humble charity of good and brotherly works. (AAS 55 1963, p. 674)

This is an observation that needs to be repeated again and again, in view of the fact that in many large cities people tend to become ''rootless,'' thus losing the sense of belonging to a parish community. There has also been a tendency for some of the basic Christian communities to live on the periphery of the parish, distancing themselves from the clergy and their fellow parishioners. However, it should be noted that the members of the 1987 Synod on the Laity did suggest that local ecclesiastical authorities should encourage the ''small, basic or so-called 'living communities', where the faithful can communicate the Word of God and express it in service and love to one another'' (cf. CL 26). They also suggested greater flexibility in the parish structure and the promotion of lay participation in parish responsibilities.

In the past, everything revolved around the pastor of the parish; he made all the decisions, ranging from the administration and maintenance of the church buildings to the scheduling of liturgical services. Now, however, canon 519 states that although the parish is entrusted to the care of the pastor, he may perform his duties ''with the cooperation of other priests or deacons and with

the assistance of lay members of Christ's faithful, in accordance
with the law.''

To what extent the laity can actively share in the duties of the
pastor is not spelled out in detail. Normally it will depend on the
bishop of the diocese — and the willingness of the pastor to
delegate some of his responsibilities to lay members of the parish.
Canon 536, however, does make provision for setting up a parish
council composed of lay members and all who are engaged in the
pastoral care of the parish. This too depends on the decision of the
bishop, who is first to consult the priests' council. That same canon
states that a parish council has only a consultative vote. On the
other hand, canon 537 calls for a finance committee to help the
parish priest administer the goods of the parish, and ''it is comprised of members of the faithful.''

The Second Vatican Council, in its document on the laity,
referred to some specific areas in which the laity should be active in
the parish: participation in the liturgical life of the parish, support-
ing and promoting the various apostolic works of the parish,
spreading the Word of God, and especially by giving religious
instruction. It also mentioned the use of ''general discussion'' to
solve various problems, and Pope John Paul II enlarged on this
point in his Apostolic Exhortation:

> The Council's mention of examining and solving pastoral prob-
> lems by general discussion 'ought to find its adequate and
> structured development through a more convinced, extensive
> and decided appreciation for Parish Pastoral Councils', on which
> the Synod Fathers have rightly insisted. (CL 27)

Unfortunately, some bishops and parish priests are reluctant
to promote parish councils. Some, perhaps, remember or have
heard of the excesses of the trustee system of years gone by,
especially in ''national'' parishes; others may be defensive and
overly protective of their clerical power and authority. Whatever

the reason, the fact is that pastoral leaders should no longer think of themselves as a privileged class, although it is certain that they do have certain responsibilities and powers that flow from the sacrament of holy orders. The proper balance between the two aspects of authority and service was nicely stated by the Second Vatican Council: "In exercising his office as father and pastor, the bishop should be with his people as one who serves, as a good shepherd who knows his sheep and whose sheep know him, as a true father who excels in his love and solicitude for all, to whose divinely conferred authority all readily submit. He should so unite and mold his flock into one family that all, conscious of their duties, may live and act in the communion of charity" (CD 16).

This statement could be applied as well to the pastor of a parish. As pastor — which means "shepherd" — he must both lead and serve; but he must keep a balance between these two functions. Too much leadership results in an exclusive authoritarianism; too much serving leads to culpable negligence. If the goal is kept in mind, namely, to form a vibrant Christian community in the parish, the pastor can avoid the extremes and, in collaborating with the laity, work effectively toward building a "communion of charity."

But there is another side to the coin. Sometimes it is the parishioners themselves who are not cooperative. Whether it is due to an extremely individualistic spirit or to an unwarranted separation between religion and daily life, many parishioners are "inactive" members of the parish community. They may attend Sunday Mass regularly, receive the sacraments and give financial support to the parish. Apart from that, they will have little or no contact with the parish staff or other members of the parish. That makes it very difficult to form the parish into a Christian community. The result is that a very small minority of parishioners become actively involved in the apostolate of the parish and they wield all the power and influence.

This is not a phenomenon peculiar to parishes; it will be found in almost any society — a family, a school, a religious community and civic organizations. Even in very democratic societies it sometimes happens that all the authority and decision-making end up in the hands of a small but powerful clique. And when this occurs, it deprives the community of the expertise and talents of those who are not members of the closed circle.

The Holy Father has called for an evangelization that will mend the "Christian fabric of society" in all parts of the world. "But for this to come about, what is needed is to *first remake the Christian fabric of the ecclesial community itself*" (CL 34). But the basic ecclesial community is the parish, and it is there that evangelization — or re-evangelization — should begin. When individual parishioners receive a solid spiritual formation they will be more likely to work toward the realization of their "primary and fundamental vocation," which is the vocation to Christian holiness. Then, as individuals or in groups and according to their condition and competence, they will be better prepared and more likely to dedicate themselves to some area of the apostolate.

We highlight the importance of spiritual formation of the individual as well as the obligation of each parishioner individually to engage in some form of apostolate, be it simply the witness to others of a good Christian life or some form of external activity. In its document on the laity the Second Vatican Council made a strong statement on this point:

> The apostolate to be exercised by the individual — which flows abundantly from a truly Christian life (cf. Jn 4:11) — is the starting point and condition of all types of lay apostolate, including the organized apostolate; nothing can replace it.

> The individual apostolate is everywhere and always in place; in certain circumstances it is the only one appropriate, the only one possible. Every lay person, whatever his condition, is called to it, is obliged to it, even if he has not the opportunity or possibility of collaborating in associations. (AA 16)

As regards the group apostolate in the parish and in the diocese, Pope John Paul II reminded the laity that their right and freedom to establish and govern associations for charitable and religious purposes "is a true and proper right that is not derived from any kind of 'concession' by authority, but flows from the Sacrament of Baptism, which calls the lay faithful to participate actively in the Church's communion and mission" (CL 29). Consequently, even at the parish level it is perfectly lawful and commendable for individuals to gather together in groups for charitable or religious purposes. There are countless opportunities for such groups to exercise a fruitful apostolate in the parish community; for example, visiting the sick, caring for the elderly and the children of working mothers, collecting food and clothing for the poor, distributing Catholic literature, etc. The activities of such groups — which constitute a needed and authentic apostolate — are something over and above the activities of the parish-sponsored groups such as the Holy Name Society or the Altar and Rosary Society.

The last word on this subject is from Pope John Paul II's document on catechesis in our time (*Catechesi Tradendae*), issued in 1979: "Admittedly, in many countries the parish has been as it were shaken by the phenomenon of urbanization. Perhaps some have too easily accepted that the parish should be considered old-fashioned, if not doomed to disappear, in favor of more pertinent and effective small communities. Whatever one may think, the parish is still a major point of reference for the Christian people, even for the non-practicing. Accordingly, realism and wisdom demand that we continue along the path aiming to restore to the parish, as needed, more adequate structures and, above all, a new impetus through the increasing integration into it of qualified, responsible and generous members" (CT 67).

THE CHRISTIAN FAMILY

Even more basic than the parish community is the family, which has been called the "domestic church." It is, as was stated by the Synod on the Laity, "the privileged place for human formation and the awakening, growth and sharing of the faith" (October 29, 1987). Yet, all is not well with family life in our contemporary society, as Pope John Paul II has pointed out: "Signs are not lacking of a disturbing degradation of some fundamental values: a mistaken theoretical and practical concept of the independence of the spouses in relation to each other; serious misconceptions regarding the relationship of authority between parents and children; the concrete difficulties that the family experiences in the transmission of values; the growing number of divorces; the scourge of abortion; the ever more frequent recourse to sterilization; the appearance of a truly contraceptive mentality" (FC 6).

In view of the evils besetting family life, it is more necessary than ever to remind the Christian faithful of the true meaning and purpose of marriage and family. Fortunately, this has been done for us by the Holy Father in his Apostolic Exhortation on the laity (1988):

> The first and basic expression of the social dimension of the person, then, is *the married couple and the family.* . . . . This partnership of man and woman constitutes the first form of communion between persons. . . .
>
> The *lay faithful's duty to society primarily begins in marriage and in the family.* This duty can only be fulfilled adequately with the conviction of the unique and irreplaceable value that the family has in the development of society and the Church herself.
>
> The family is the basic cell of society. It is the cradle of life and love, the place in which the individual "is born" and "grows." Therefore a primary concern is reserved for this community,

especially in those times when human egoism, the anti-birth campaign, totalitarian politics, situations of poverty, material, cultural and moral misery, threaten to make these very springs of life dry up. Furthermore, ideologies and various systems, together with forms of uninterest and indifference, dare to take over the role in education proper to the family. . . .

It is above all the lay faithful's duty in the apostolate to make the family aware of its identity as the primary social nucleus, and its basic role in society, so that it might become always a more *active and responsible* place for proper growth and proper participation in social life. In such a way the family can and must require from all, beginning with public authority, the respect for those rights which, in saving the family, will save society itself. . . .

As experience testifies, whole civilizations and the cohesiveness of peoples depend above all on the human quality of their families. For this reason the duty in the apostolate towards the family acquires an incomparable social value. The Church, for her part, is deeply convinced of it, knowing well that ''the path toward the future passes through the family.'' (CL 40)

The foundation of the family is the conjugal union that is effected by the spousal love of husband and wife. And this marital love is in turn the origin and source of family life, because everything in marriage flows from the mutual love of the spouses. This was stated by Pope John Paul II in his Apostolic Letter for the International Year of Youth (1985): ''To set out on the path of the married vocation means to learn married love day by day, year by year: love according to soul and body, love that is 'patient, is kind, that does not insist on its own way... and does not rejoice at wrong, . . . love that rejoices in the right, love that endures all things' (1 Cor 13:4-7). . . . It is precisely this love that you young people need if your married future is to 'pass the test' of the whole of life. And precisely this test is part of the very essence of the vocation which, through marriage, you intend to include in the plan of life'' (AAS 77 (1985), pp. 620-621).

Marriage cannot be thought of simply in relation to the exchange of vows at the wedding ceremony; rather, like ordination to the priesthood and the final profession of religious vows, it is the commitment of one's entire life, ''until death.'' For that reason husbands and wives should be mindful of the fact that the graces of the sacrament of matrimony are available to them during the entire course of their married life. And since the marital relationship is the most intimate sharing that is possible between human beings, all the more reason why the man and woman who give their lives and their love to each other should at the start have as much in common as possible.

The conjugal act whereby the husband and wife become ''two in one flesh'' is not only a sexual experience of intense pleasure; much more than that, it should be a total gift of self to the other as an expression of generous love. So Pope John Paul II, in his Encyclical on the family, wrote: ''Sexuality, by means of which man and woman give themselves to one another through the acts which are proper and exclusive to spouses, is by no means something purely biological, but concerns the innermost being of the human person as such. It is realized in a truly human way only if it is an integral part of the love by which a man and a woman commit themselves totally to one another until death'' (FC 11).

The Holy Father then adds that ''this totality, which is required by conjugal love, also corresponds to the demands of responsible fertility. This fertility is directed to the generation of a human being, and so by its nature it surpasses the purely biological order and involves a whole series of personal values'' (FC 11). Therefore, when they become parents, the husband and wife take on new relationships, new responsibilities and a new kind of love: parental love. This is then the authentic ''basic Christian community'': father, mother and children constituting the domestic church. It is a community formed by love and for love. Indeed, as the Holy

Father asserts: "Without love the family is not a community of persons, and in the same way *without love the family cannot live, grow and perfect itself as a community of persons*" (FC 18). Therefore, the surest guaranty that a family will be an authentic Christian community is the mutual gift of love between the husband and wife. When the children sense that their parents truly affirm and serve one another with unselfish love, they are in fact receiving the primary education in what constitutes Christian community.

When we speak of the Christian family as an area of apostolate, we should note that there is an apostolate within the family — of members to one another — and there is an apostolate beyond the confines of the home. Within the family, according to biblical teaching, the father should exercise headship and authority; he should love and cherish his wife; he should provide for his family by his daily work; he should affirm his children with love and apply the discipline they need for growth in virtue.

The duties of the mother are to be a helpmate and partner to her husband, to manage the household and to be the primary educator of her children. It is therefore important for a mother to place a priority on home and family as long as her children need her presence and her loving care. And if, for a serious reason the mother must work outside the home while her children are still young, whoever acts as her proxy in caring for the children should be selected with extreme care.

Another element in the apostolate internal to the family is the interaction of the members of the family with each other in the domestic circle. St. Rose of Lima compared community life to a sculptor's studio. After he has completed the sculpting of a statue, he polishes it with an abrasive material to make the rough edges smooth. Something similar happens in family life. Members of the family soon learn that the peace and harmony of the home can be maintained only by the practice of certain basic social virtues. Frequently an individual must give up his or her personal preferences for the good of the family as a whole. At other times it is necessary to endure patiently the tensions that inevitably arise in domestic life. In this way family life can serve as a ''novitiate'' or apprenticeship for Christian maturity.

The second aspect of the family apostolate proceeds directly from the virtues that have been cultivated in the domestic circle. Pope John Paul II develops this aspect of family apostolate in his Encyclical on the Christian family. This document, incidentally, should be read by all parents and by those contemplating marriage:

> The family has vital and organic links with society, since it is its foundation and nourishes it continually through its role of service to life; it is in the family that citizens come to birth and it is within the family that they find the first school of the social virtues that are the animating principle of the existence and development of society itself.
>
> Thus, far from being closed in on itself, the family is by nature and vocation open to other families and to society, and undertakes its social role.
>
> The very experience of communion and sharing that should characterize the family's daily life represents its first and fundamental contribution to society. . . .
>
> Thus the fostering of authentic and mature communion between persons within the family is the first and irreplaceable school of social life, an example and stimulus for the broader community relationships marked by respect, justice, dialogue and love. . . .
>
> Families therefore, either singly or in association, can and should devote themselves to manifold social service activities, especially in favor of the poor, or at any rate for the benefit of all people and situations that cannot be reached by the public authorities' welfare organization. (FC 42)

In the words of the Holy Father, the family is "a believing and evangelizing community; a community in dialogue with God; and a community at the service of man" (FC 51).

PUBLIC LIFE AND THE PROFESSIONS

Our emphasis on the temporal or secular order as the proper sphere of the lay apostolate must be repeated again when we discuss the role of the Christian laity in public life, in the professions and in the work place. In the document on the Church in the modern world the Second Vatican Council uses unusually strong language when treating of the relationship of the lay Christian to society:

> The pace of change is so far-reaching and rapid nowadays that no one can allow himself to close his eyes to the course of events or indifferently ignore them and wallow in the luxury of a merely individualistic morality. The best way to fulfill one's obligations of justice and love is to contribute to the common good according to one's means and the needs of others, even to the point of fostering and helping public and private organizations devoted to bettering the conditions of life. There is a kind of person who boasts of grand and noble sentiments and lives in practice as if he could not care less about the needs of society. . . .

> Let everyone consider it his sacred duty to count social obligations among man's chief duties today and observe them as such. For the more closely the world comes together, the more widely do men's obligations transcend particular groups and gradually extend to the whole world. This will be realized only if individuals and groups practice moral and social virtues and foster them in social living. Then, under the necessary help of divine grace, there will arise a generation of new men, the molders of a new humanity. . . .

> It is to the laity, though not exclusively to them, that secular
> duties and activity properly belong. When, therefore, as citizens
> of the world, they are engaged in any activity either individually
> or collectively, they will not be satisfied with meeting the
> minimum legal requirements but will strive to become truly
> proficient in that sphere. . . . It is their task to cultivate a properly
> informed conscience and to impress the divine law on the affairs
> of the earthly city. . . .
>
> The laity are called to participate actively in the whole life of the
> Church; not only are they to animate the world with the spirit of
> Christianity, but they are to be witnesses to Christ in all
> circumstances and at the very heart of the community of man-
> kind. (GS 30 and 43)

As regards public life, Pope John Paul II has stated that the
laity must never relinquish their participation in the economic,
legislative and social areas of public life (CL 42). It would be
difficult to overestimate the need to incorporate Christian values at
all levels of public life in the contemporary world. By the same
token it would be difficult to exaggerate the power and influence —
for good or for evil — of men and women in public office. And this
is true on both the national and the international level. When we
look at the world through the news reports on television and in the
press, we are brought face to face with the serious social injustices
that stifle freedom, violate human rights, and keep a large portion
of the human race in a state of poverty and misery.

After their 1971 Synod on justice in the world the bishops
issued a document in which they listed the various forms of injustice and oppression that plague the human race. They then made
a plea for the recognition of the United Nations Declaration of
Human Rights by all nations, the support of the United Nations as
an instrument for peace among nations, and an increase of help by
the rich nations to the developing countries. But the bishops
realized that governments are run by individuals, and hence the

urgent need for changing the method of education which in our day "encourages narrow individualism" and "exalts possessions." Rather, "educational methods must be such as to teach men to live their lives in its entire reality and in accord with the evangelical principles of personal and social morality which are expressed in the vital Christian witness of one's life" (CU III).

This same topic was addressed by the 1987 Synod in its "Message to the People of God": "Socio-political commitment presupposes a solid formation, proportionate to the level of present and future civic responsibilities. Above all, this commitment must be anchored in the principle of coherence between the life of faith and political and social activities. In this way we bring to social structures and activities the spirit of the Gospel" (October 29, 1987).

Bishop Paul J. Cordes of the Pontifical Council on the Laity offers some helpful insights in his book *In the Midst of Our World*:

> The task of working jointly for the construction of society and the well-being of daily life by fostering the dignity of the human person and the value of culture is essentially the duty of the laity. . . . We need to preserve or strive toward spheres of freedom in which Christian life can be lived. Yet it is only to be expected that many attempts by individuals or by groups to do so will end in failure, because the secularized environment in which they necessarily operate will crush them. When this happens, Christians must not lose hope; they must be patient and long-suffering; they must not be discouraged in their commitment. Failure is not a catastrophe. The action of God's Spirit is not bound to external signs or particular places. Indeed, these signs and places may even be a stumbling block themselves. . . .
>
> Many things that appear to people as crosses are, in fact, abuses against which our reaction is necessary. We must strive, by protest and resistance, to change them. Yet, in the last analysis, the Cross cannot be removed or eradicated from human life. Any

system of coordinates in which no room is left for the Cross as a basis for our judgment and action must be rejected. When difficulties or disasters strike at us or at others, we must at least try to give them some meaning; they are the means of bringing redemption, and even though beyond our grasp or inaccessible to our experience, they bring grace and salvation. . . .

It is the duty of Christians too to create righteousness and justice in the world. How this can be achieved, and how we can play a part in it, often, however, remain beyond our insight. Faith alone can sustain our hope in an eternal reward. (pp. 126-128)

Some forms of the apostolate call for a specialized training and in many countries the government agencies have drawn up specific legislation and regulations, especially in the area of health education and social services. There are countless professional men and women in specialized fields who have much to contribute to the overall mission of the Church. Indeed, they are in many cases the persons in the best position to change the world for the better by practicing their professions according to Gospel values. Therefore, the Second Vatican Council rightly called for the establishment of institutions of higher learning and the provision of courses in theology in schools for professional training (GE 9).

We cannot stress too strongly the importance of a Christian education for men and women in the various professions. We may feed the poor, clothe the naked and give shelter to the homeless, but in order to abolish social injustices and defend human rights, it is necessary to provide a solid moral formation for those who will one day be civic leaders. It is therefore counterproductive to promote "free schools" for the poor at the expense of the so-called "private schools" for students preparing for professional careers. We need both, of course, but with the current emphasis on "justice and peace," it is necessary sometimes to defend the very existence of Catholic institutions of higher learning. In their "Message to the People of God" the bishops of the 1987 Synod stated that a "sense of Christian involvement should bring lay people into the fields of health, culture, science, technology, work and the means of social communication'' (October 29, 1987).

People are often more readily influenced — for good or for evil — by those with whom they have professional or family ties. That is why the apostolate of ''like toward like'' is so important and also why professionals as well as workers in the various trades should be encouraged to group together, not only for economic gain, but to work for the common good of society.

Many lay people live in two different worlds. Like the ''church-on-Sunday'' Catholic, they divorce their religious beliefs and moral values from their daily life and work. This is especially regrettable when professional people live and work this way, because they are in such a pivotal position for promoting moral values and for exerting an influence on others. Society and the Church need doctors and nurses, judges and lawyers, politicians and diplomats, teachers and artists, businessmen and journalists who in their daily life will witness to their faith and will refuse to compromise on Gospel principles.

ASSOCIATIONS OF THE LAITY

Before we discuss the various movements and associations comprised of the lay faithful, we should take note of the remarks of Pope John Paul II concerning the collaboration of men and women in the mission of the Church. In his Apostolic Exhortation to the laity the Holy Father mentions a problem that is known to all but discussed by few: ''excessive insistence given the status and role of women'' can lead to the omission of sufficient reference to men:

> In reality, various sectors in the Church must lament the absence
> or the scarcity of the presence of lay men, some of whom
> abdicate their proper church responsibilities, allowing them to

be filled only by women. Such instances are participation in the liturgical prayer of the Church, education and, in particular, catechesis of their own sons and daughters and other children, presence at religious and cultural meetings, and collaboration in charitable and missionary initiatives.

Therefore the coordinated presence of both men and women is to be pastorally urged so that the participation of the lay faithful in the salvific mission of the Church might be rendered more rich, complete and harmonious.

The most common and widespread way, and at the same time, fundamental way to assure this coordinated and harmonious presence of men and women in the life and mission of the Church, is the fulfillment of the tasks and responsibilities of the couple and the Christian family. (CL 52)

It should be no surprise, however, that many men "abdicate" their responsibilities in the apostolate and let them be "fulfilled only by women." The same thing sometimes happens in the family, when the father leaves most of the domestic management and family decisions to the mother. When it comes to church activities, and especially those pertaining to the liturgy, men are notorious for hanging back. Since the Second Vatican Council and with the restoration of the permanent diaconate perhaps men in the future will be less reluctant to assume their obligations in the life and mission of the Church.

Another factor that may help to remedy the situation is the gratifying multiplication of lay movements and associations in the Church during the past few decades. In its document on the laity the Second Vatican Council highly endorsed the various forms of group apostolates for the laity. They correspond to the social needs of the laity and they manifest the Church as a community of believers. Moreover, many apostolates by their very nature require the concerted effort that can be provided only by a group or an association. Consequently, says the Second Vatican Council, "wherever the laity are at work, the apostolate under its collective and organized form should be strengthened" (AA 18). At the same time it is necessary to remind the members of apostolic movements and associations that they "are not ends in themselves; they are meant to be of service to the Church's mission to the world. Their apostolic value depends on their conformity with the Church's aims, as well as on the Christian witness and evangelical spirit of each of their members and of the association as a whole" (AA 19).

There is an urgent need for lay men and women in the various apostolates of the Church, particularly in view of the fact that many of the activities that were performed by priests and religious have been neglected or abandoned. We think, for example, of catechetical instruction, teaching in Catholic schools, care of the sick and various social services. Meanwhile, some religious have opted to work in apostolates that are more properly the responsibility of the laity. Perhaps the Church also needs more volunteers, or at least workers who are willing to serve the Church for a just but more moderate salary. The 1971 Synod of Bishops had something to say in this regard:

> Our examination of conscience now comes to the lifestyle of all: bishops, priests, religious and lay people. In the case of needy peoples it must be asked whether belonging to the Church places people on a rich island within an ambient of poverty. In societies enjoying a higher level of consumer spending, it must be asked whether our lifestyle exemplifies that sparseness with regard to consumption which we preach to others as necessary in order that so many millions of hungry people throughout the world may be fed. (CU III)

When lay movements with a predominantly spiritual purpose first began, some of them met with criticism. They were accused of withdrawing too much from the world to a highly individualistic —

if not self-centered — spirituality. Moreover, when Pope Paul VI addressed an international charismatic congress in Rome, he reminded them of their duty to love and serve their neighbor and to be obedient to the pastors of the Church. In other instances some of the lay movements distanced themselves too much from the life of the parish or diocese. Yet that was to be expected as the laity took their first faltering steps toward greater autonomy and self-government.

Today we can point with great satisfaction to various lay movements and associations, some old and some new, that are promoting the mission of the Church. It is somewhat risky to make any kind of a list, but we mention the following as examples that come to mind: St. Vincent de Paul Society, Knights of Columbus, Serra Club, Legion of Mary, Opus Dei, Marriage Encounter, Christian Family Movement, Communion and Liberation, Movement for a Better World, Basic Christian Communities, and Focolare.

As we have seen, the *Code of Canon Law* affirms the freedom of the laity to form and govern their own independent organizations. Pope John Paul II followed this up by listing certain criteria by which lay movements and associations are to be evaluated:

> *The primacy given to the call of every Christian to holiness.* . . .
> In this sense whatever association of the lay faithful there might
> be, it is always called to be more of an instrument leading to
> holiness in the Church, through fostering and promoting "a
> more intimate unity between the everyday life of its members
> and their faith." (AA 19)

> *The responsibility of professing the Catholic faith.* . . . For this
> reason every association of the lay faithful must be a *forum*
> where the faith is proclaimed as well as taught in its total content.

> *The witness to a strong and authentic communion* in filial rela-
> tionship to the Pope . . . and with the local Bishop . . . and in
> *"mutual esteem for all forms of the Church's apostolate"*

(AA 23). The communion with Pope and Bishop must be expressed in loyal readiness to embrace the doctrinal teachings and pastoral initiatives of both Pope and Bishop. Moreover, Church communion demands both an acknowledgment of a legitimate plurality of forms in the associations of the lay faithful in the Church and at the same time, a willingness to cooperate in working together.

Conformity to and participation in the Church's apostolic goals, that is, "the evangelization and sanctification of humanity and the Christian formation of people's conscience, so as to enable them to infuse the spirit of the Gospel into the various communities and spheres of life" (AA 20). From this perspective every one of the group forms of the lay faithful is asked to have a missionary zeal which will increase their effectiveness as participants in a re-evangelization.

A commitment to a presence in human society. . . . Therefore, associations of the lay faithful must become fruitful outlets for participation and solidarity in bringing about conditions that are more just and loving within society. (CL 30)

The Holy Father then lists the fruits that are produced by the various lay movements and associations: "the renewed appreciation for prayer, contemplation, liturgical and sacramental life; the reawakening of vocations to Christian marriage, the ministerial priesthood and the consecrated life; a readiness to participate in programs and Church activities at the local, national and international levels; a commitment to catechesis and a capacity for teaching and forming Christians; a desire to be present as Christians in various settings of social life and the creation and awakening of charitable, cultural and spiritual works; the spirit of detachment and evangelical poverty leading to a greater generosity towards all; conversion to the Christian life or the return to Church communion of those baptized members who have fallen away from the faith" (CL 30).

During the 1987 Synod of Bishops representatives from all over the Catholic world presented what they considered to be the priorities in the present-day apostolate of the Christian faithful: apostolate of the Christian family, ministry to children and youth, revitalization of parish life, evangelization of mission countries, apostolate to the working class, and greater concern for the Christian formation and continuing education of the laity. It was also suggested that the existing Pontifical Council for the Laity should be raised to the status of a Congregation, since there are already Congregations for the Clergy and for Consecrated Life. Finally, in view of the repeated insistence of the Second Vatican Council and the *Code of Canon Law* that the proper field for the lay apostolate is the world and the temporal order, lay men and women who want to participate in the Church's mission should not think first or exclusively of being asked to perform liturgical or sacramental ministries.

CHAPTER 5

SPIRITUALITY OF THE LAITY

The word "spirituality" needs a definition because it is not a word that is commonly used by ordinary Christians; in fact, some of them may feel uncomfortable with it. Yet it is a term that is coming more and more into common usage since the Second Vatican Council. It is not at all unusual to find any number of recently published books that treat of Christian spirituality in general or the spirituality of a particular saint or religious institute. What is unusual is the fact that in January, 1988, the magazine *Better Homes and Gardens* published a "Spirituality Report" in which the first question asked was: "Do you think spirituality is gaining or losing influence on family life in America?" Incidentally, 50% of the respondents said yes, and 33% thought that it was losing, while 14% thought it was remaining stable.

In times past the average lay Christian considered spirituality to be the exclusive domain of the clergy and religious, except for a few rare cases of saintly lay men and women. Consequently, any member of the laity who wanted to become a truly holy and dedicated Christian would have to enter a convent or monastery or, at the very least, to separate oneself as much as possible from the affairs of the world. But that is — and has always been — an erroneous idea. This is evident from the words of Christ himself, who addressed this statement to the multitude: "You, therefore, must be perfect, as your heavenly Father is perfect" (Mt 5:48).

And St. Paul repeated the same teaching: ''It is God's will that you grow in holiness'' (1 Th 4:3); ''To all in Rome, beloved of God and called to holiness'' (Rm 1:7).

We could cite numerous passages from the writings of saints and spiritual authors throughout the centuries, all of whom emphasize the universal vocation of all the Christian faithful to holiness. For our purposes, however, it suffices to quote the teaching of St. Francis de Sales, who stands without equal as a theologian for the laity:

> Almost all those who have hitherto written about devotion have been concerned with instructing persons wholly withdrawn from the world or have at least taught a kind of devotion that leads to such complete retirement. My purpose is to instruct those who live in town, within families, or at court, and by their state of life are obliged to live an ordinary life as to outward appearances. Frequently, on the pretext of some supposed impossibility, they will not even think of undertaking a devout life. It is their opinion that . . . no one should aspire to the palm of Christian piety as long as he is living under the pressure of worldly affairs. I shall show such men that . . . a strong, resolute soul can live in the world without being infected by any of its moods. (*Introduction to the Devout Life*, Preface)

> It is an error, or rather a heresy, to wish to banish the devout life from the regiment of soldiers, the mechanic's shop, the court of princes or the home of married people. It is true, Philothea, that purely contemplative, monastic life and the devotion of religious cannot be exercised in such states of life. However, besides those three kinds of devotion there are several others adapted to bring perfection to those living in the secular state. . . . Wherever we may be, we can and should aspire to a perfect life. (*Introduction to the Devout Life*, Part I, no. 3)

What St. Francis de Sales means by the devout life is what we are talking about when we discuss spirituality. It has to do with living one's faith and becoming more and more aware of one's incorporation into Christ through the sacrament of baptism. Put in another way, it means a conscious striving for the sanctification and holiness that are the goal of the Christian life. In his intervention at the 1987 Synod on the Laity, a Bishop from the Netherlands echoed the sentiments of St. Francis de Sales: "Let us propose a notion of sanctity which is the opposite of the invitation to leave this world as it is and to look for union with God elsewhere. Let us formulate a notion of holiness which makes us aware of God's presence within this world and this history of ours. Accepting God's call to holiness, we become more realistic . . . because it is God's efficacious presence which guarantees the ultimate sense of all we perform, suffer, enjoy and hope." (*Bulletin of the Bishops' Synod*, October 9, 1987).

Since the promulgation of the Second Vatican Council's document on the Church, no Catholic can be ignorant of the fact that "all the faithful, whatever their condition or state — though each in his own way — are called by the Lord to that perfection of sanctity by which the Father himself is perfect" (LG 11). With so much insistence in the past on receiving the last sacraments and dying in the state of grace, it is easy to see why some Christians are not sufficiently aware of their duty to *live and grow* in grace and holiness. This is readily verified by the answers we could expect to the question: "Are you saved?" The committed Christian Protestant would most likely respond: "Yes, I am saved, because I have accepted Jesus Christ as my personal Savior." The Catholic will answer: "I don't know; I'm not dead yet."

CHRISTIAN SPIRITUALITY

In its widest sense spirituality simply means the living of one's faith. Consequently, any person who believes in the transcendent being that we call God, and lives according to that belief, will manifest a particular spirituality, regardless of his or her religion. In this context we may rightly speak of a Jewish or Muslim spirituality as well as a Christian spirituality. Moreover, according to the Second Vatican Council: "The Catholic Church rejects nothing of what is true and holy in these religions. . . . Yet she proclaims and is duty bound to proclaim without fail, Christ who is the way, the truth and the life" (NA 2).

When, therefore, we speak of *Christian* spirituality, we are talking about faith in Jesus Christ and a conscious experience of union with him through prayer and a life lived in conformity with his teaching. The ideal, of course, is to be configured to Jesus Christ through faith and baptism, to grow in grace and charity to Christian maturity, and to witness to Christ according to one's state of life and personal gifts and talents.

Faith is the first requirement in any religion, like ours, that is based on a deposit of revealed truths. Hence the question often asked by Jesus: "Do you believe?" If we believe that Jesus Christ is the Son of God and speaks in the Father's name, we can confidently accept and follow his teaching. According to the Gospel, faith in the teaching of Christ should then lead to repentance, conversion and baptism. And Christ assures us that through the baptism of water and the Holy Spirit we are born again as children of God in the life of the Spirit. "In this the love of God was made manifest among us," says St. John, "that God sent his only Son into the world, so that we might live through him" (1 Jn 4:9).

Together with the gift of sanctifying grace, by which we share in the very nature and life of God himself (2 P 1:4), we receive the power to fulfill the twofold precept of charity: to love God above all things and to love one another as Jesus loved us. And here we touch on the very essence of Christian holiness and Christian spirituality. So St. Augustine says: "Love God, and do what you will; you will not sin"; and St. John of the Cross states: "In the evening of life, you will be judged by love."

But the love that is charity is a special kind of love; it is not simply a more intense and generous human love. It is a supernatural virtue infused with sanctifying grace and hence it is a gift from God. Does this mean that charity is so different from human natural love that they are opposed to each other, that it is somehow un-Christian to love oneself? Love of self, or self-preservation, is the first law of nature, and therefore it is perfectly legitimate because, as St. Thomas Aquinas teaches, grace does not destroy nature but works through it to perfect it. The only type of love that is opposed to and would in fact destroy grace and charity is a seriously sinful love that would be totally incompatible with the love of God and neighbor. That is why we can say that every sin springs from a disordered self-love.

Charity, however, is a love that transcends self in order to go out to the "other," whether that other be God or our neighbor. Rather than a "need" love, it is a "gift" love, or what St. Thomas Aquinas calls "friendship love." It is further characterized in Scripture as a marital or spousal love or a parental love, because those kinds of love best portray the loving relationship that should exist between ourselves and God and with our fellow Christians.

In chapter 13 of his First Epistle to the Corinthians St. Paul lists the various fruits that proceed from the love that is charity. They are, in effect, Christian virtues that should be practiced by the disciples of Christ. For that reason St. Thomas Aquinas states that the supernatural virtue of charity, which is infused into the soul together with sanctifying grace, is the motivating power of all the other Christian virtues. Indeed, the supernatural virtues depend so much on charity that, except for faith and hope, they cannot exist without it. Moreover, there is a pattern of virtues that corresponds to each state of life or vocation and this is an important consideration when speaking of the spirituality and holiness of individuals. Married persons will need to cultivate a set of virtues quite distinct from the unmarried person; the virtues of the diocesan priest will not be the same as those living the consecrated life; indeed, there are also specific virtues that are proper to the doctor and nurse, the lawyer and judge, the teacher and the soldier.

But above all these things one must have charity in order to be truly holy. That is why we say that charity is the very essence of Christian perfection and that it is not what we *do* that makes us holy, but the *love* with which we do it. Unfortunately, some Christians do not understand this doctrine sufficiently and as a consequence they concentrate on some aspect of Christian living that is only secondary. In his biography of St. Francis de Sales, Bishop Jean Pierre Camus (1652) quotes the saintly Bishop of Geneva as follows:

> Some place their virtue in austerity; others in abstemious eating practices; some in almsgiving, others in frequenting the sacraments of penance and the Eucharist; another group in prayer, either vocal or mental; still others in a certain sort of passive and supereminent contemplation; others in those gratuitously given, extraordinary graces. And all of them are mistaken, taking the effects for the causes, the brook for the spring, the branches for the root, the accessory for the principal, and often the shadow for the substance. For me, I neither know nor have experienced any other Christian perfection than that of loving God with all our heart and our neighbor as ourselves. Every other perfection without this one is a false perfection.

This does not mean, of course, that one can ignore the cultivation of the virtues other than charity. We have already stated that every Christian has an obligation to practice the virtues that are required for the proper fulfillment of his or her duties of state in life. St. Francis de Sales treats of this in his *Introduction to the Devout Life*:

> In practicing the virtues we should prefer the one most conformable to our duties rather than one more agreeable to our tastes. . . . Every state of life must practice some particular

virtue. A bishop's virtues are of one kind, a prince's of another, a soldier's of a third kind, and those of a married woman are different from a widow's. All men should possess all the virtues, yet all are not bound to exercise them in equal measure. Each person must practice in a special manner the virtues needed by the kind of life he is called to. (Part III, no. 1)

By this time we should no longer be tempted to think of "Christian spirituality" as some extraordinary phenomenon that marks the lives of saints and mystics but is alien to the lives of "ordinary Christians." We should also be convinced that all of the faithful of Christ without exception are called to holiness or, as was stated by the Second Vatican Council, "to the fullness of Christian life and to the perfection of love." The more intense our actual love of God and neighbor, and the more that love prompts us to perform the acts of virtue proper to our state of life, the more we shall advance along the road to perfection. It is not a question of receiving extraordinary gifts and graces, nor is it a question of performing exceptional and difficult works. Rather, as St. Teresa of Avila said, it is a question of doing ordinary things extraordinarily well. We repeat: It's not what you do that makes you holy, but the love with which you do it. For that reason the same Saint advised that we should work as if it all depended on us and then pray as if it all depended on God.

The perfection of charity is the goal toward which we should strive, and that perfection is attained through the faithful and conscientious performance of the duties of one's state of life under the impetus of love of God and of neighbor. Therefore the saintly Christian is not necessarily characterized by exceptional gifts and talents, by extraordinary accomplishments, or by separation from the world and the society of other people. There are, however, certain general means that are available to all the faithful of Christ who want to grow in grace and holiness.

MEANS FOR SPIRITUAL GROWTH

Incorporated into Christ through baptism, Christians receive through that sacrament the sanctifying grace that makes them children of God and the supernatural virtue of charity by which they can establish the loving relationship with God that constitutes Christian holiness. Unfortunately, although the waters of baptism wash away all stain of sin, there still remain in the baptized Christian the effects of original sin. We have a wounded nature and for that reason we experience the tension between the desire for greater perfection and the various temptations that come to us from the world, the flesh and the devil. If, in addition, an individual has compounded the difficulty by yielding to temptation, it is necessary to repent of one's sins, to do penance and to amend one's life. And the process of conversion will be all the more difficult if one has cultivated strong habits of sin. Hence the importance of avoiding sin and the occasions of sin. Anything in the life of a Christian that is an obstacle to growth in the love of God and neighbor should be resolutely overcome.

If grace and charity are to reach their full expansion and intensity in the life of the Christian, it is necessary to make use of the positive means that are available to all the faithful. These means have traditionally been listed as: the worthy reception of the sacraments, the cultivation of the virtues proper to one's state of life, and the practice of prayer. And it should be noted at the outset that the most efficacious means is the worthy reception of the sacraments. The reason is that the sacraments infallibly produce grace in the souls of those who receive them with the proper dispositions.

THE SACRAMENTS

Since the Second Vatican Council the Vatican has issued more documents and instructions on the liturgy and the sacraments than on any other subject. The reason for this is that it is "of the greatest importance that the faithful should easily understand the sacramental signs, and should eagerly frequent those sacraments which were instituted to nourish the Christian life" (SC 59). Therefore, all apostolate and ministry, including the lofty mission of preaching the Gospel, should lead the faithful to the sacraments. "For the goal of apostolic endeavor is that all who are made sons of God by faith and baptism should come together to praise God in the midst of his Church, to take part in the Sacrifice of the Mass and to eat the Lord's Supper" (SC 9).

In receiving the sacrament of baptism the Christian makes a commitment to the way of life proposed by Christ and receives all the spiritual powers necessary to follow that way with all fidelity. The sacrament of confirmation is something of a "personal Pentecost" or a special sending of the Holy Spirit to reaffirm the vocation of every Christian to share actively in the Church's mission. The sacrament of penance reconciles the sinner to God and bestows the grace to resist future temptations, for which reason it should be received frequently. Those who truly love God can never repeat too often that they are sorry for their sins. Then, reconciled to God, they can worthily receive and be spiritually nourished by the Body and Blood of Christ in the sacrament of the Eucharist. This sacrament, too, should be received frequently; in fact, as long as they are properly disposed, the faithful are encouraged to receive Communion when they attend Mass. Finally, at one time or another the individual Christian needs the strength and comfort that come through the sacrament of anointing. "Extreme unction, which may also and more fittingly be called the 'anointing of the sick,' is not a sacrament for those only who are at the point of death. Hence, as soon as any one of the faithful begins to be in danger of death from sickness or old age, the appropriate time for him to receive this sacrament has certainly already arrived'' (SC 73).

In discussing the two remaining sacraments — matrimony and holy orders — we are dealing with sacraments that have a social orientation. The sacrament of holy orders confers the priesthood of Christ on those who receive it. It is called ''ministerial'' priesthood because all priests are ordained for ministry to the People of God, and this ministry takes three distinct forms: ministry of the word (preaching the Gospel and teaching religious truths), ministry of the sacraments (the cultic and liturgical aspect of priestly ministry), and ministry of leadership and government (the formation and guidance of the Christian community at the diocesan or parish level). Like all other Christians, the bishops and priests are called to the perfection of charity and they sanctify themselves by the very works of their ministry.

The sacrament of matrimony has its origins in the biblical account of the creation of the first man and woman. The Book of Genesis has two different descriptions of creation: Genesis 1 to 2:4a and Genesis 2:4b to 2:25. In the first account, human beings, both male and female, are created on the ''sixth day'' and are given dominion over everything that God had created on the previous five days. The second account is much more detailed; man is created first, and then the various animals, ''but none proved to be the suitable partner for the man'' (2:20). So the Lord ''cast a deep sleep on the man, and while he was asleep, he took out one of his ribs and closed up its place with flesh. The Lord God then built up into a woman the rib that he had taken from the man.'' When God presented the woman to the man, he accepted her as his partner or helpmate.

These two accounts are ''pre-scientific,'' but they contain a divine message concerning the vocation of man and woman to mutual love, partnership and conjugal fruitfulness through procreation. It is interesting to note in passing that even today some Arabs will speak of a close and intimate friend as their "rib" (cf. S.B. Clark, *Man and Woman in Christ*, Ann Arbor: Servant Books, 1980, p. 18). In any case, God is the author of marriage and Christ raised that natural covenant of love to a sacrament.

As a covenant of love between man and woman, marriage necessarily involves the conjugal union that is of its nature ordained to the procreation of children. But, as Pope John Paul II has stated in his document on the Christian family: "Sexuality, by means of which man and woman give themselves to one another through the acts which are proper and exclusive to spouses, is by no means something purely biological, but concerns the innermost being of the human person as such. It is realized in a truly human way only if it is an integral part of the love by which a man and a woman commit themselves totally unto one another until death." (FC 11).

In an address delivered in November, 1979, the Holy Father stated that "the first and immediate effect of marriage is the Christian conjugal bond." Later, in his document on the Christian family (1981), the Pope says:

> The love between husband and wife and, in a derivative and broader way, the love between members of the same family . . . is given life and sustenance by an unceasing inner dynamism leading the family to ever deeper and more intense *communion*, which is the foundation and soul of the *community* of marriage and family.
>
> The first communion is the one which is established and which develops between husband and wife; by virtue of the covenant of married life, the man and woman "are no longer two but one flesh" and they are called to grow continually in their communion through day-to-day fidelity to their marriage promise of total mutual self-giving.
>
> This conjugal communion sinks its roots in the natural complementarity that exists between man and woman, and is nurtured through the personal willingness of the spouses to share

their entire life-project, what they have and what they are; for
this reason such communion is the fruit and the sign of a profoundly human need. But in Christ the Lord, God takes up this
human need, confirms it, purifies it and elevates it, leading it to
perfection through the sacrament of Matrimony; the Holy Spirit,
who is poured out in the sacramental celebration, offers Christian couples the gift of a new communion of love that is the living
and real image of that unique unity which makes of the Church
the indivisible Mystical Body of the Lord Jesus. (FC 18-19)

It is, therefore, the conjugal loving union between husband
and wife that represents the union between Christ and his Church,
as described by St. Paul (cf. Ep 5:22-33). And it is this conjugal
union that is "the foundation on which is built the broader communion of the family, of parents and children, of brothers and sisters
with each other, of relatives and other members of the household"
(FC 21).

The Virtues

The cultivation of the virtues proper to one's state of life
serves as a means for growth in perfection and holiness in a variety
of ways. First of all, any virtuous action that is motivated by the
supernatural virtue of charity can produce an increase of sanctifying grace and a more intense love of God and of neighbor. Secondly, although the love that is charity is the essence of Christian
perfection, the various virtues serve as expressions and manifesta-
tions of one's love of God and of neighbor. Thirdly, all of the
faithful should strive to reach Christian maturity, and this is
achieved only when the individual personality has been integrated
and stabilized by the pattern of virtues proper to one's state of life
or vocation.

The eminently Christian virtues are the theological virtues of faith, hope and charity; and the greatest of these three is the virtue of charity. By faith we believe in God and accept as true all that he has revealed; as a result, we can transcend the limitations of human knowledge and fix our gaze on that which lies beyond the horizon of the present world. By the virtue of hope we can trust that God will fulfill his promises if we in turn cooperate with the graces he offers us; consequently, we can rid ourselves of any excessive attachment to the things of this world, since we know that our true home is above. With the virtue of charity we are able to love God above all things and to love our neighbor as a fellow-traveler toward eternal life and glory; we are thus able to resist the vehement demands of self-centered love and re-direct that love, as it were, toward God and neighbor.

When, however, we speak of the virtues as means for growth in Christian holiness, we are referring especially to the *moral* virtues. We can, of course, increase our faith, hope and charity, but it is the moral virtues that relate most directly to the formation of a mature, adult personality. The reason for this is that grace and the theological virtues operate through the human personality, and it is especially by means of the moral virtues that we form a mature and integrated personality. Every human action that is performed with sufficient awareness and consent is a "moral" action; that is, in the concrete it is either morally good or morally evil. And one who habitually performs any morally good action is said to possess the virtue or good habit that pertains to that type of activity. Conversely, anyone who habitually performs a morally evil act is said to have that particular vice. Unfortunately, there are usually two vices confronting each virtue, because virtue "lies in the middle." To put it another way, any extreme — whether too much or too little — is usually a sin or a vice, or at least an imperfection. The key to a virtuous life is moderation.

Both the ancient Greek and Roman philosophers and the later Christian theologians have selected four basic virtues to which all other virtues can somehow be related. This was not only helpful in teaching but it was also a way of discovering the basic virtues that are needed for a morally good life and some degree of maturity. These virtues are four in number: justice, temperance, prudence and fortitude.

And where does one begin to cultivate the virtues that are necessary for a good Christian life? The moral formation of the individual begins in the very first years of life, in the home and family. For that reason the 1987 Synod on the Laity stated in its ''Message to the People of God'':

> The Christian family, founded on the sacrament of marriage, is the privileged place for human formation and the awakening, growth and sharing of the faith. May it become a true ''domestic Church'' where its members pray together, live the commandment of love in an exemplary way, and life is welcomed, respected and protected. (October 29, 1987)

Psychologists of religion have stressed the importance of moral formation in the family setting. Gordon Allport, for example, contends that the single most important influence on the development of religious sentiment in a child is the religion of the mother, and especially a mother who prays. ''There is considerable evidence,'' says Allport, ''to show that the most religious-minded adults were raised by parents who themselves were deeply religious. It is not that children of pious parents always accept the doctrinal position in which they were trained. Very often they rebel against parental orthodoxy, and yet the sincerity of their parents' outlook has profoundly influenced them'' (*The Individual and His Religion*, p. 31).

Again the question: where does one begin? If we look back at our own moral formation, most of us would find that the first training we received was in the area of justice: rights and duties. The importance of justice in personal and social life is immediately evident; it is the application of the first principle of morality: "Do good; avoid evil." In the social life of the family a child soon learns that there are duties to be performed and rights of others to be respected. Consequently, there are limits and restrictions on one's freedom. The Second Vatican Council described the family as "the first school of those social virtues which every society needs" (GE 3). And Pope John Paul II has stated that: "Children must be enriched not only with a sense of true justice, which alone leads to respect for the personal dignity of each individual, but also and more powerfully by a sense of true love, understood as sincere solicitude and disinterested service with regard to others, especially the poorest and those in most need. . . . And the communion and sharing that are part of everyday life in the home at times of joy and at times of difficulty are the most concrete and effective pedagogy for the active, responsible and fruitful inclusion of the children in the wider horizon of society" (FC 37).

When the child reaches puberty and enters the difficult stage of adolescence, it is physiologically ready for marriage and parenthood, which is the natural vocation of man and woman. For many young people this is a period of stress, not only because of sexual confusion and tension, but because the time has come to think of leaving the family nest, the control of parents, and to become a responsible member of society. In some cases there may be a rebellious reaction against parental authority and a deep questioning of previously held religious doctrines and moral values. But this is all part of putting away the things of a child and becoming an adult.

However, since nature herself has prepared the adolescent for marriage and parenthood, it is essential that youth should "receive a positive and prudent education in matters relating to sex" (GE 1). And this sex education, "which is a basic right and duty of parents, must always be carried out under their attentive guidance, whether at home or at educational centers chosen and controlled by them. . . . In view of the close links between the sexual dimension of the person and his or her ethical values, education must bring the children to a knowledge of and respect for the moral norms as the necessary and highly valuable guarantee for responsible personal growth in human sexuality. For this reason the Church is firmly opposed to an often widespread form of imparting sex information dissociated from moral principles'' (FC 37).

Obviously, sex education should be adapted to the needs of the child or the adolescent. Too often the manuals of sex education explain and illustrate sexual matters that are too far advanced for the child. Answers are given to questions that the child has not even asked. As a result, says Pope John Paul II, it is "an introduction to the experience of pleasure and a stimulus leading to the loss of serenity — while still in the years of innocence — by opening the way to vice'' (FC 37). Parents, who have the first responsibility for the education of their children, would do well to read the *Declaration on Certain Problems of Sexual Ethics*, issued by the Sacred Congregation for the Doctrine of the Faith in 1975.

The use and enjoyment of sex is restricted to men and women who are married to each other. Within that context the conjugal act is, or ought to be, a mutual self-giving that expresses the love of the spouses for each other; it is therefore a morally good action. As St. Thomas Aquinas puts it: "Pleasure enjoyed in a good action is good; pleasure enjoyed in a bad action is evil." But the sensual pleasure that is enjoyed in food, drink and sex is often so intense that one can easily go to excess in the area of sensate satisfaction. For that reason it is necessary to cultivate the virtue of temperance.

Temperance can signify either a general characteristic or a special moral virtue. As a general characteristic it is simply the moderation that every mature Christian should practice in accordance with reason enlightened by faith. This is necessary not only for achieving a balanced and integrated personality but also for good health. As a special virtue, temperance controls the inclination to the sensate pleasure derived from food, drink and sex in accordance with one's state of life. All human instincts, functions and pleasures are good in themselves and many of them have a noble function and purpose. Therefore, any moral evil attached to these things will have to come from the individual person; for example, the unlawful or excessive use and enjoyment of these things, the manner of performing a pleasurable action (in accordance with or contrary to the nature of the act), or the motive for performing the pleasurable act.

Nature herself provides us with instinctive dispositions that are controlling factors of sensual pleasure, and especially of sexual pleasure. St. Thomas Aquinas refers to the "sense of shame" and the "sense of honor," and it is important that parents and educators should respect and cultivate these dispositions in those who are committed to their charge. Dr. Conrad Baars offered the following prudent advice to those in charge of the sexual education of the young, and especially the parents:

> In the growing years all questions about sex should be answered honestly and simply, but without detailed explanations. Young children especially are satisfied with much more simple answers than their questions may indicate. Premature descriptions of the mechanics of sex could be as harmful and inhibiting as awkward, ill-timed parent-child sex talks which, because of the obvious embarrassment of the parent, convey only too forcefully the impression that there is something wrong with sex and that there is little or no chance to deal with it in a natural manner, not even when grown-up and married. Parents who find these talks embarrassing do much better to give their children a reputable book which they can read in privacy. (*Sex, Love and the Life of the Spirit*, p. 53).

Of all the moral virtues, the most important is the virtue of prudence. It is the virtue that marks maturity and adulthood; it is also the virtue that serves as the fulcrum for all the other moral virtues, because persons lacking prudence can never be sure that they will act virtuously under given circumstances. By definition it is the virtue that enables the individual to perform the morally good action under present circumstances and in view of the ultimate end. Consequently, the development and perfection of the virtue of prudence will depend to a large extent on the formation of conscience, which is the faculty by which we make moral judgments.

There are three acts involved in the exercise of prudence: deliberation, judgment and execution. Deliberation means that we should think before we act. Depending on the importance or the complexity of the contemplated action, one must consider the various means for attaining an end or the ways of performing the action. Once the matter has been deliberated, a choice must be made, and this is the function of judgment. Finally, the decision or choice is carried out when the will gives the command to act or refrain from acting.

In order to cultivate the virtue of prudence it is also necessary to acquire certain qualities or dispositions of character. First of all, it is necessary to have a basic understanding of the moral principles that govern human actions and the ability to reason logically so that one may apply those principles to particular circumstances. Secondly, one must have a good memory in order to learn from experience; and if experience is lacking, the individual should have the docility to learn from others and to take their advice. Hence the importance of good models for the young and inexperienced. Thirdly, before carrying the decision into action, it is important to look again at the special circumstances surrounding the contemplated action and to look ahead at the possible consequences of the action in question.

Since prudence is the virtue that marks maturity and therefore relies heavily on experience, we do not presume that young people or beginners in any field or profession will possess a high degree of this virtue. There are exceptions, of course, but normally the inexperienced should not be placed in important positions of decision and government. By the same token, parents and educators should give special attention to the formation of the young, fostering those qualities or dispositions that are the marks of maturity. Moreover, one can see the importance of a novitiate, apprenticeship, pastoral training or internship to prepare people for their state of life or profession. Experience is the teacher of prudence.

We come at last to the fourth of the basic moral virtues: the virtue of fortitude. At first glance one would think that this is a virtue that is proper to the young and the strong, and, indeed, to men only. That is a popular misconception, based on the fact that aggressiveness is usually attributed to men and, consequently, most of our heroes are men of action. As a matter of fact, the Latin word for virtue (*virtus*) also means fortitude or strength, and it is derived from the Latin word for man (*vir*). If, however, we read the ancient classics of Greece and Rome and some of the dramas of Shakespeare, we discover that, unlike the Hollywood productions, the heroes usually die. "The coward dies a thousand times; the hero dies but once."

Actually, the virtue of fortitude comes into play in the face of an impending danger. If the danger can be faced and overcome, then fortitude is exercised by courageously advancing toward the danger in order to defend oneself against harm or death. But if there is no escape from the threatening danger or present suffering, the virtue of fortitude enables the individual to endure with patience and perseverance what cannot be overcome or avoided. "What can't be cured, must be endured." And it is much more difficult to do this than to strike out at an opponent with reckless courage, largely because aggressive action is usually preceded and accompanied by anger. But to hold to the good, firmly and undaunted, whatever the pain and suffering, sometimes calls for a strength of soul that is sheer heroism.

We have treated of fortitude last of all because it is a virtue that is progressively more necessary as we approach the peak of our powers and then face the inevitable fact that death awaits us all. Of course, dangers and difficulties are part of every person's life, from childhood to old age, and therefore the Christian needs to exercise fortitude throughout his or her life. But it is especially when our strength and powers begin to fail, when sickness comes, and when our last hour approaches that we need the support and the tranquility of the virtue of fortitude to overcome our fear and anxiety.

Perhaps we shall have an even greater awareness of the need to cultivate the four basic moral virtues if we recall how each one of them contributes to the formation of the Christian character. Justice is the foundation for the love of neighbor that Christ commands us to practice; temperance enables us to observe the rule of reason in moderating our enjoyment of sensate pleasure; prudence gives us the practical wisdom we need in order to live as mature Christians; fortitude helps us to imitate Christ in patiently bearing the crosses of life.

THE PRACTICE OF PRAYER

One of the most evident characteristics of the spirituality that has emerged since the Second Vatican Council is the predominant place given to the practice of prayer. It is true that immediately after the promulgation of the document on the liturgy, with emphasis on active participation in liturgical functions and the promotion of community prayer, some misguided enthusiasts rejected all forms of personal, mental prayer and all private devotions. That led to what the French theologian, Jacques Ellul called "theological lies": "Your work is your prayer; loving your neighbor is prayer"; and even distorting the Benedictine motto to read: "*Orare est laborare.*"

Fortunately there has been a return to the orthodox understanding of prayer as well as a willingness to acknowledge the various forms or grades of prayer. Whether one thinks of prayer as "conversation with God, who loves us" (St. Teresa of Avila), or "raising the mind and heart to God" (St. John Damascene), or "the language of love" (St. Thomas Aquinas), it is certain that the object of prayer is God. It is therefore an act of religion as well as an expression of our love of God. And it is so important for spiritual life and growth that without the regular practice of prayer an individual may easily lose his or her taste for the things of God and the practice of religion.

Spiritual writers, like St. Teresa of Avila, St. Ignatius Loyola and St. Francis de Sales, who have written on the practice of prayer, usually divide the various types of prayer into stages or "grades of prayer." As with any other spiritual practice, there are types of prayer that are proper to beginners, to the advanced and to the perfect. Moreover, there is a basic division of prayer, just as there is for the spiritual life in general; namely, the division into *ascetical* prayer and *mystical* prayer. The word "ascetical" applies to all those exercises of the spiritual life in which we exert the effort to cooperate actively with the graces that God gives us. The word "mystical," on the other hand, designates any activity or experience in which we are receptive of God's action upon us; in other words, we are led by the Holy Spirit rather than being the primary agents of our own actions. This can occur in any stage of one's spiritual development if the Holy Spirit so wills and if the individual is moved by an intense love of God and a total abandonment to the divine will.

As regards the practice of prayer, it suffices for our discussion to list the following grades of prayer: vocal prayer, meditation, affective prayer and contemplative prayer. Normally one begins with the practice of vocal prayer and then, if he or she remains faithful to prayer, there should be a progression through the other and higher types of prayer. This does not mean that every individual will reach the higher stages of contemplative prayer, however, because those degrees of prayer are mystical; they depend more on God's choice than on our efforts.

Vocal prayer is any form of prayer that is expressed in words, whether written or spoken. It may be private or public, personal or communal; for example, the public liturgical prayers in which the faithful participate are something quite different from the private recitation of the "Our Father" or the reading of a litany from a prayer-book. In both cases vocalized prayer, says St. Thomas Aquinas, is very commendable because it arouses interior devotion, it renders homage to God with our mind as well as our heart, and it enables us to give external expression to our religious sentiments of adoration, contrition, petition and thanksgiving.

Public liturgical prayer of the People of God gives greater glory to God than does private prayer and it has greater efficacy because it is a community prayer. "Where two or three are gathered in my name, there am I in their midst" (Mt 18:20). Yet, considering the very nature of prayer and the person who prays, the higher stages of prayer will be more contemplative and personal. Jesus said: "When you are praying, do not behave like the hypocrites who love to stand and pray in synagogues or on street corners in order to be noticed. I give you my word, they are already repaid. Whenever you pray, go to your room, close your door, and pray to your Father in private. Then your Father, who sees what no man sees, will repay you" (Mt 6:5-6).

Jesus then continued with his instruction on vocal prayer: "In your prayer do not rattle on like the pagans. They think they will win a hearing by the sheer multiplication of words. Do not imitate them. Your Father knows what you need before you ask him" (Mt 6:7-8). It can easily happen that when reciting the words of a prayer, especially a prayer known by memory, such as the "Our Father" or "Hail Mary," we are simply babbling words. St. Teresa of Avila warned her nuns about this:

> That prayer which does not attend to the one it is addressing and what it asks and who it is that asks and of whom it asks, such I do not call prayer at all, however much one may move the lips. (*The Interior Castle*, First Mansions, Book 1, Chap. 7)

> When people tell you that you are speaking with God by reciting
> the Paternoster and thinking of worldly things — well, words fail
> me. When you speak, as it is right for you to do, with so great a
> Lord, it is well that you should think of who it is that you are
> addressing, and what you yourself are, if only that you may
> speak to him with proper respect. (*The Way of Perfection*, Chap.
> 22)

Besides attention, it is also necessary to pray with devotion;
that is, to direct one's will and sentiments to God. This is so
important that it would be more beneficial to recite one "Our
Father" with great devotion than to recite numerous prayers in a
routine and distracted fashion. The reason for this is that it is not
what we do — or say — that makes us holy, but the love with which
we do it. This should be a consolation to those whose daily duties
do not allow them much leisure time for personal prayer; it is also
an endorsement of the brief pious utterances or ejaculations that
one can address to God throughout the day.

When, however, a person has formed a strong habit of practicing daily prayer, the prayer itself will gradually become more
internalized and the individual will find it easier to be recollected in
times of prayer. Usually the individual will then begin to practice
what is called "discursive meditation," which is the first grade or
stage of mental prayer. It is a kind of spiritual rumination or
reflection on some spiritual truth that increases one's love for God
and enables one to live more and more in the divine presence.

There are many methods proposed for the practice of meditation, but whether a person uses the simplified Carmelite method or
the more complicated meditations outlined by St. Ignatius Loyola
and St. Francis de Sales, any discursive meditation involves three
acts: consideration, application and resolution. In the first act a
person selects some spiritual topic — for example, a scene or event
in the life of Christ or some particular virtue — and thinks about it
in order to understand what it means. Having done this, one applies

the spiritual topic to oneself, asking what significance it has to one's life here and now. Finally, in the third act, the individual asks what he or she is going to do about it, and this should lead to some kind of resolution. St. Teresa of Avila thought that discursive meditation was so beneficial that if a habitual sinner were to start this practice, he or she would soon give up sin or give up meditating.

It should be evident from our description of discursive meditation that it is an invaluable aid in the cultivation of the virtues and the formation of a Christian character. Moreover, as a type of mental prayer it brings into play the virtue of prudence which, as we have seen, is also composed of three elements: think, judge, act. As a matter of fact, in making a discursive meditation we are focusing our attention on ourselves to a great extent because we are applying spiritual truths to our own lives with a view to improvement. And incidentally, it would seem that the prayer best suited for children is vocal prayer, but when they reach adolescence, the transitional stage between childhood and adulthood, they should be encouraged to practice some type of discursive meditation. The reason should be obvious: adolescents are at the threshold of young adulthood and should therefore be thinking of their vocation in life and then forming the virtues needed in view of that vocation.

The second stage of growth in the practice of mental prayer is reached when a person's prayer is truly the language of love. This is called "affective" prayer and was greatly promoted by St. Francis de Sales. It is really a very simplified form of recollection in which love and the affections play a dominant role. Some persons are by nature so affectionate and responsive that they very quickly enter upon this stage of prayer. The distinctive aspect of affective prayer is that, whereas in discursive meditation the individual concentrates largely on self in order to become a good Christian, in affective prayer the focus is on God who is loved. Therefore the passage to the practice of affective prayer marks a profound transition in the orientation of one's life.

However, spiritual writers such as St. Teresa of Avila and St. John of the Cross warn against certain dangers that should be avoided. First of all, one should never use force or constraint in order to arouse the affections. Secondly, since affective prayer is usually accompanied by spiritual consolations, those who are easily stimulated to movements of affection may think they are at a much higher stage of perfection than they actually are. Thirdly, since spiritual consolations are extremely gratifying, one may unwittingly be seeking self-satisfaction and thus practicing prayer for the consolations and satisfaction it provides. That is why St. John of the Cross warns against seeking oneself in God instead of seeking God in oneself.

We come last of all to contemplative prayer, which may be acquired through the faithful practice of prayer or infused supernaturally by God. The former type of contemplative prayer is an ascetical type of prayer; the latter is mystical. One will find in books on the spiritual life that a variety of names have been used to designate "acquired contemplation": prayer of simplicity, loving awareness of God, prayer of divine presence, prayer of simple regard, gaze of love and, perhaps, centering prayer. Some of these names were coined because of a fear of or an aversion to the word "contemplation." But in reality contemplation is no more strange or esoteric than a mother's loving gaze fixed upon her child, the esthetic experience of the beautiful in the fine arts, or the reflective and peaceful enjoyment of a beautiful sunset. Anyone who truly appreciates the beautiful already has a predisposition to experience contemplative prayer.

In this stage of prayer, even more than in affective prayer, the individual is drawn to God as the object of his or her love, and to such an extent that the individual gradually and painlessly becomes more and more detached from created things. As one moves toward more intimate union with God, he or she will inevitably move away from the things of earth. There is at the same time an ever-increasing forgetfulness and disregard for self as the individual fixes his or her interior gaze on God and moves more and more rapidly toward union with him. Although one's spiritual journey is at first slow and halting, at a snail's pace, the soul now feels like an eagle, flying into the face of the sun. The more closely the soul approaches the "divine magnet," the faster it moves.

Such are the grades of prayer which lead to the supernatural, mystical stages of prayer that are the domain of the Holy Spirit. In a strict sense we cannot make a neat division or separation between ascetical and mystical prayer on the level of experience. The Spirit "breathes where he will." As we have already noted, a person in the lower stages of the spiritual life may, because of the total abandonment of self to God through love, be lifted up by the Spirit. On the other hand, a soul that has experienced lofty grades of mystical prayer may find it necessary at times to return to the lower, ascetical practices of prayer. Once again, the axiom of St. Teresa: "Work as if it all depended on you, and pray as if it all depended on God."

HOLINESS OF THE LAITY

We have stated previously that the vocation of the laity has a double aspect: they are called to personal holiness and they are called to participate actively in the Church's mission. Ideally the lay apostolate should flow from personal holiness and at the same time the laity should sanctify themselves by the very works of their apostolate. Pope John Paul II has stated: "Holiness, then, must be called a fundamental presupposition and an irreplaceable condition for everyone in fulfilling the mission of salvation within the Church" (CL 17).

But the apostolate that is proper and distinctive of the laity is one that is carried on in the midst of the world and secular affairs. Therefore the spirituality and holiness of the laity must be fostered and developed by their daily activities in domestic, professional and social life. "The vocation of the lay faithful to holiness," says the Holy Father, "implies that life according to the Spirit expresses itself in a particular way in their *involvement in temporal affairs* and in their *participation in earthly activities*" (CL 17).

Given the necessary distinction between lay spirituality and that of the priesthood and the consecrated life, we can logically expect that the spirituality of the laity will have its own proper characteristics. And so it does, although in many respects the theology of lay spirituality is still in process and not yet completed. Nevertheless, we can enumerate certain trends and aspects that have emerged in the last few decades.

Lay spirituality is incarnational rather than eschatological. Traditional spirituality emphasized the world to come, life after death and personal salvation. Detachment and separation from the things of the world were postulated as conditions for living a holy Christian life, particularly for those living the evangelical counsels in the religious life, which is characterized in a special way by "separation from the world." Some spiritual writers even branded the world as evil. Contemporary spirituality, on the contrary, looks on the world and temporal realities as something good, created by God and given to humanity for its use and governance. Without denying that created things can be occasions of sin for those who use them evilly, the challenge to Christians today is to "have the Gospel spirit permeate and improve the temporal order" (AA 2).

Lay spirituality is secular rather than monastic. As long as one makes separation from the world an essential ingredient of Christian spirituality, the laity will continue to harbor the false notion that holiness is reserved to priests and religious. It will not be easy to disabuse them of this notion as long as spiritual writers and preachers continue to exalt the celibate and contemplative life to such an extent that the active life and marriage are held in low esteem. Fortunately, the Second Vatican Council has placed before the whole Church the teaching of Christ, that all his followers are called to perfection, and that this vocation to holiness stems from the very fact of their baptism. Consequently, ''lay spirituality will take its particular character from the circumstances of one's state in life (married and family life, celibacy, widowhood), from one's state of health and from one's professional and social activity. Whatever the circumstances, each one has received suitable talents and these should be cultivated, as should also the personal gifts he has received from the Holy Spirit'' (AA 4).

Lay spirituality is one of involvement rather than withdrawal. The precept of charity is twofold: love of God and love of neighbor. However much an individual may be drawn to the contemplative state of life, this is not the path that leads to holiness for the laity. This is not to say that the higher stages of contemplative prayer are beyond the reach of the laity; it is quite evident that many of them actually do receive this gift from God. But in view of the fact that some persons may be tempted to withdraw from the duties of their lay state in life, the Second Vatican Council has stated:

> All that goes to make up the temporal order: personal and family
> values, culture, economic interests, the trades and professions,
> institutions of the political community, international relations,
> and so on, as well as their gradual development — all these are
> not merely helps to man's last end; they possess a value of their
> own, placed in them by God. . . . This natural goodness of theirs
> receives an added dignity from their relation with the human
> person, for whose use they have been created. . . . Laymen . . .
> while meeting their human obligations in the ordinary conditions
> of life should not separate their union with Christ from their
> ordinary life; but through the very performance of their tasks,
> which are God's will for them, actually promote the growth of
> their union with him. (AA 4)

Beginning with the domestic circle of the family and extending to the neighborhood and parish, the Christian laity have ample opportunity — and a duty — to be involved with others. ''The human person," says Pope John Paul II, "has an inherent social dimension which calls a person from the innermost depths of self to *communion* with others and to the *giving* of self to others" (CL 40).

Lay spirituality is community oriented rather than individualistic. In one sense, the spiritual life begins and ends with the person; we come into the world alone and we go out alone. And even in the context of community, there is a sense in which we can say that the most important element in any community is the individual person. Nevertheless, the Holy Father has said that "all that is accomplished in favor of the person is also a service rendered to society, and all that is done in favor of society redounds to the benefit of the person" (CL 40). Hence the great emphasis today on the concept of community and the formation of so many new groups and movements to encourage a common sharing in the life and mission of the Church.

Lay spirituality is apostolic rather than contemplative. This in no way militates against the practice of prayer by the laity. We have already discussed the importance of personal mental prayer for all Christians in every state of life. Rather, the emphasis is once again on the obligation of the laity to participate actively in the mission of the Church. Pope John Paul II put it this way: "The vocation to holiness is *intimately connected to mission* and to the responsibility entrusted to the lay faithful in the Church and in the world. . . . The eyes of faith behold a wonderful scene: that of a countless number of lay people, both women and men, busy at work in their daily life and activity, oftentimes far from view and quite unacclaimed by the world, but nonetheless looked upon in love by the Father" (CL 17). The laity have been called to the apostolate and for that reason the name "Catholic Action" was suitably applied to the role of the laity in the mission of the Church. Dag Hammarskjold once said: "In our age the road to holiness necessarily passes through the world of action." And how many there are who need the loving care and service of devout Christians: children and youth, the aged, the homeless, the sick, the poor, persons suffering from various addictions, the underprivileged, those suffering from racial or economic injustice. It is in these areas of apostolic action that the laity can perfect themselves in the charity — love of God and neighbor — that is the essence of Christian holiness. At the same time, these apostolic works are sermons in action, that show the world what it means to be a disciple of Christ.

At the close of the 1987 Synod on the Laity the bishops addressed their "Message to the People of God," which concluded with this appeal:

> You peoples of the world who are wounded in your dignity, attacked in your freedom, despoiled of your possessions, persecuted because of your religious faith, delivered up without just defense to the capricious will of powers of every imaginable kind, we want to tell you that the Church is close to you; it wants to be among you and with you, as a witness to the liberating love of Christ, who frees us and reconciles us with the Father.

> You who are abandoned and pushed to the edges of our consumer society; you who are sick, people with disabilities, poor and hungry, migrants and prisoners, refugees, unemployed, abandoned children and lonely old people; you who are victims of war and all kinds of violence inflicted by our permissive society, we say that the Church shares your suffering. It takes it to the Lord, who in turn associates you with his redeeming Passion. You are brought to life in the light of his Resurrection. We need you to teach the whole world what love is. We will do everything we can so that you may find your rightful place in the Church and in society.

> You, our human families: We exhort you to appreciate your vitality and greatness. Christian families, be the 'domestic churches' where men and women open themselves to the love of God and to their brothers and sisters.

You, our young men and women: You carry on your shoulders the hopes of the world and the Church. Do not allow yourselves to be frightened by the world you see. Do not allow your dynamism to be destroyed by an apathy that comes from an easy life. Look to Christ, who is the Way, the Truth and the Life, who is youth to the new humanity. He will be for you the source of a life that creates a more just and loving world.

Women: You justly fight for the full recognition of your dignity and your rights. May this struggle give birth to a world of dialogue, a world where man and woman complement each other, as willed by the Creator. He entrusted to us our personal destinies which we, as men and women, are called upon to work out. Finally, he gave to the Church the woman restored in the fullness of her femininity and grace, Mary, the Virgin.

We turn to you, you who carry in your hands the destiny of peoples and nations, you who hold the keys of wealth and power, you who plan the opportunities and the happiness of men and women with a view to a better world; you who accumulate the powers of destruction, you who are men and women of science, culture and art. We are aware of how great your responsibilities are and how often the path of action is not clear. The world needs peace. Men and women must be respected in their fundamental rights. The life of every human person is sacred. We count on you to defend life, as we assure you of our prayers so that you may realize your difficult task. If you possess the smallest measure of authority it is to put yourselves at the service of the human person and not to enslave it.

Bishops, priests and deacons: Let us form living communities 'assiduous in the teaching of the Apostles, the community of the faithful, in the breaking of the bread and in prayer' (Ac 2:42). Let us receive and accept the gifts of the Spirit in the lay faithful, and let us stimulate the sense of communion and responsibility.

Brothers and sisters in Christ: Let us live our vocation to holiness, each of us where he or she is; and all of us together in the community of the faithful. Let us respond with generosity to the appeal of Christ: 'Go, teach all nations' (Mt 28:19). All of us are missionaries.

Christians of all denominations: Let us advance on the road of unity willed by Christ: 'That all may be one' (Jn 17:21).

Believers and men and women of good will: Let us join hands to build a world of justice and peace.

All of you, men and women, young and old, children of every condition of life, sick and the elderly, priests, men and women religious who open new paths and bring the world to come nearer; you who form links of fraternity, harmony, justice and peace: The Church recognizes itself in you and tells you never to lose courage, since 'hope never deceives' (Rm 5:15).

LaVergne, TN USA
28 September 2009
159155LV00011B/1/P